THE INCOMPLETE ANGLERS

JOHN D. ROBINS

The Incomplete Anglers

All rights reserved. No part of this publication may be reproduced, stored, or introduced into a retrieval system or transmitted in any form by any means, electronic or mechanical, including photocopying, recording, or otherwise, without prior written permission of the copyright owner, except for brief passages quoted by a reviewer.

Originally published in December, 1943, and reprinted in February, 1944 and in October, 1944, by Wm. Collins & Sons Co. (Canada) Ltd. Illustrations were done by Franklin Carmichael, R.C.A., O.S.A., who planned the entire book and directed its typography.

Second edition reprinted in 1998 by The Friends of Algonquin Park, Box 248, Whitney, Ontario K0J 2M0, (613) 637-2828, with permission from the Copyright Board of Canada.

Printed and bound in Canada by Custom Printers of Renfrew Ltd., Box 415, 25 Argyle St. N., Renfrew, Ontario K7V 4A6

ISBN 1-895709-44-X

Net proceeds from the sale of this book will help further the work of The Friends of Algonquin Park (a non-profit, charitable organization dedicated to enhancing the educational and interpretive programs in Algonquin Park since 1983).

CONTENTS

		PAGE
	FORECAST	1
I.	OUR SETTING OUT	5
II.	PACK AND PADDLE	19
III.	ON THE TRAIL, PARDNER	57
IV.	AT THE FORKS	73
V.	A RAINY DAY	97
VI.	THE ROCK CAMP	115
VII.	THE CAMP AT LAVIEILLE DAM	141
VIII.	THE CAMP ON LAKE LAVIEILLE	159
IX.	ON THE LAKES	181
X.	THE ISLAND OF THE PINES	201
XI.	ALL OVER	217

FORECAST

THERE HAS been much writing on fishing, most of it intended both for instruction and delight. It is a pleasing evidence of the fundamental humility of the craft that all fishermen are delighted with instruction. But the fisherman, with all his humility, has a deep-seated abhorrence of mediocrity, which for him is worse than failure. Now this abhorrence is closely connected with loyalty to the fish themselves. Two instances of non-success a man willingly recounts—his inability to obtain a single rise and his inability to land a certain fish. He tells the first of these because it involves a glad recognition, if not a proud parade, of the intelligence and personality characteristic of game fish in general; the second because it is a tribute to the size and prowess of certain fish in particular. But mediocrity, the taking of moderate catches of moderate fish, is, as I said, abhorrent, and hence unmentionable. No fisherman would write about such catches. On the other hand, a whole book cannot be written about fish which did not rise, or about fish which got away. The inevitable and logical result, often slanderously misinterpreted, has been that only successful anglers write. There have been no 'prentice anglers among the writers; nay, there have been no journeymen, but only masters, fit to wag the beard with Isaak Walton. Anglers with the itch to write have always been anglers with the right to itch, by virtue of their skill in angling.

Moreover, in these later times there have been many books concerned with fishing in streams and lakes remote from men, and more remote from women. Here the emphasis may shift from the gallant struggle or the fickle coyness of the shadowy trout to the rigours of the long portage. But the common and inadequate man is denied participation still. Perfection of expertness is not always claimed in this latter kind of fishing story, but perfection of equipment takes its place. To judge by these accounts, no one ventures to invade the wilds but sportsmen, men well able to afford the service of a corps of guides, men with dainty eighty-dollar rods and sybaritic cots. Or, if not perfection of equipment, then perfection of manhood. For there is another type which roams the literary bush. He is the strong wordless hero, who carries with him but one shirt, one pair of socks, one trouser, and thus defies The Forest. But even he, except in melodrama, has a guide; *ergo*, an income.

In the chronicles and treatises of those who fish in quiet waters among the haunts of men, and of those who paddle and portage their way into the haunts of deer and moose, there are then no imperfect men. All are men who in themselves are heroes, who through patient decades have learned the mysteries of the cast, or whose personalities have been mechanically expanded by the gadgets of the sporting stores, at the price of a king's ransom, and who command as well the minds and muscles of super-guides.

But these are not the only men who fish in distant waters. There are those of the feebler sort, who cast a fly (when they do not cast a worm) in faith, hoping that it will light at some distance from them, and within fair distance of the growing circles that show where a trout has risen, but with no reasonable expectation that it will do so. There are those who do not know a Parmcheenee Belle from a Montreal, once they have taken it from the labelled fly-card, and who yet dare to fish, and—what's more—who get 'em. There are men who go to the woods to camp and fish, and who must forgo a new suit of clothes to do it; men who must go unguided if they are to go at all, and who hence must also go uncotted; men whose tackle is so meagre as to be contemptible. There are men who go into the forest to holiday, so unheroic that they tire on a three-mile carry, so unfitted for canoeing that they cannot even swim, so effeminate that they must have two shirts if possible, and must sleep within a flytoxed tent, not underneath the everlasting stars, or dripping clouds, as may be.

I know that there are such, for I am one. Moreover, there is at least one more, for he was with me. I think I have met here and there on narrow trails with still others who were even like unto us. For such as these I set down the doings of two incomplete anglers in the moderately northern woods.

I know that your great artist, even the reminiscent fishing artist, is at his best when he is not hampered by the dullness of sober history. But the plodder dare not allow himself this liberty. When he lies, he is at once detected by the shallowest wit, and his only safety lies in the truthfulness of his record. Therefore this is to all intents and purposes a story of the actual.

This actuality is a fishing and canoeing trip made by two men into Algonquin Park in the Province of Ontario, the first of a series which we hope is not yet ended. I am

FORECAST

not sure to what extent our experiences have been typical, wherefore I have not tried to eliminate the purely personal, since I do not know how exclusively personal it may be. The reader will encounter food lists and perhaps at times a hortatory tone. The presence of both lists and tone is to be explained by the author's early reading in the subject. The camping narrative that most stirred his youthful imagination abounded in both.

OUR SETTING OUT

CHAPTER I

THE NOMINAL leadership of our expedition was mine. Tom, while not a stranger to the bush, had never been on a canoe trip. I had taken quite a number, but I had learned little. I owed my rank chiefly to a man named Jim, for, while Jim did not initiate me into camping, he did take me to the Park, and he did introduce me to the Fly, and my superiority really depends on these two advantages. I know that a self-respecting fly would cut me dead, but it could not deny that we have met. Jim, moreover, taught me to regard the Grub List as a sacred scripture. He made me acquainted with the Tump, which I had always reverenced afar. I may say that nowadays I sometimes take a tump-line with me, but it is solely for effect. I have used it for as long as eight to ten minutes, to impress Tom. I doubt if he has even noticed it. Other debts I owe to Jim, who is a practised canoeist and fisherman, an incurable romantic, and knows the President of the Toronto Anglers' Club quite well. He explains my dignity, therefore, because he is the third factor in our proportion. I was to Tom, poor wretch, as Jim is to me. Had I written of some earlier trip with Jim, I should have been cast in my proper rôle of duffer-narrator. This account is, of course, merely a variation on that popular theme, with two duffers instead of the customary one.

A bit of winter correspondence had begun the arrangements. Tom was to arrive in Toronto in the early morning of the twelfth of June. I was to have the shopping all done. By this means we should be able to start out by nine o'clock at the latest, drive merrily to North Bay, store the car, and catch the night transcontinental for Radiant, in the Park itself.

This plan miscarried on account of Tom's instincts, which are usually dependable, and which were in this case supremely sound. They told him, or perhaps preliminary reading of sports literature told him, that a canoe trip begins when you buy for it. Now both Tom and I have the ordinary man's dislike of household or personal buying, but shopping for the bush is very different. (The standard term, I suppose, is *outfitting*, but our expenditure was so modest that I scarcely feel justified in using the more resplendent expression.) Not only is it a joy to buy, but there is also a pleasant reminiscent thrill each time the gradually tattering brown paper is wrapped once more around the bacon in the bush. Therefore I sighed but sympathized when a last-minute note from Tom suggested that I should postpone the buying until he arrived. I sighed because I realized that we should not be able to set out before half-past eleven, possibly twelve o'clock. Actually, of course, it was after three when we turned out of the driveway.

You will be spared the full account of our buying, chiefly because the anticipatory joys and the fragrant glamour of camp shopping would be communicated only to those familiar with it, and will be communicated to them just as well by the Grub List itself. To others it would seem as insipid, as lacking in bouquet, as yesterday's newspaper.

Our important purchases were made in two stores, the first a mighty giant whose stride takes in a continent and the islands thereof, from which we bought our groceries and meats. I say meats because, as will appear, we took chipped beef, half a pound, in addition to bacon. The second store snuggles for companionship in a row of little shops. It can be recognized afar by the curious crowd of men and boys perpetually changing places in front of one window, where turtles and lizards and mice and snakes display their charms.

There is a most tactful young man in this little hive, a hive whose bait-boxes dot the camp-sites and the fishing spots of half the North. When I say "the North" I really mean the southern part of Northern Ontario. It deceives no one, and allows me quite cheaply and quite harmlessly some of the thrill of traversing Great Bear Lake with Mackenzie or Kelsey or somebody. For aught I know, the hive's bait-boxes do dot the remote camp-sites of this farther North. I cannot say, for I myself have never dotted them nor crossed the Great Bear Lake, except in daydreams. But I was speaking of this salesman's tact. I have gone into sporting-goods establishments to buy a nickel's worth of sinkers, and so obviously to buy a nickel's worth of sinkers that the haughty dukes of the emporium have left me standing timidly for twenty minutes, until my courage oozed, and I walked seven blocks to buy them happily and proudly from the young man in the hive—and in addition, half a hundred flies I didn't need.

At this present time of writing I have some idea of the flies I wish to buy. I know that for our pet stream the

Silver Doctor is my own reliable. I know that for us the Montreal is good, and the Professor useful, and the McGinty and the Cow Dung, and sometimes the Caddis Dark. But this first year of independent fly purchase, this year of our chronicle, I bought by the books. That is to say, I bought flies for the aesthetic appeal of their names, or because of some half-forgotten association with certain fishing essays of my youth, when fly-fishing smacked of pious elegance and literary dilettantism, of Dr. Henry Van Dyke, who by an unpardonable anachronism always has for me a pointed beard. For instance, I have a perfectly useless supply of Parmcheenee Belles. I have never caught anything on a Parmcheenee Belle, except an overhanging bough, but to this day, under that ancient spell, I add a few each time I buy. Latterly, the name had been shortened, perhaps under the influence of golf, to the uneuphonious Par Belle. Had it been called by that name always, I should never have bought one. Hackles, too, have had a glamour for me, especially the Red Hackle. Until I looked it up, five minutes ago, I did not know what a hackle was, but it suggested wild Scottish moors and streams to me. The Royal Coachman, though self-explanatory, and therefore without mystery, was tempting. So that day I took any whose names I happened to remember, a few because they looked as if they should be attractive to fishes, and some half-dozen on the recommendation of the young man.

We bought one hundred dew-worms, neatly housed in a moss-filled, burlap-covered box, a plague to carry on the trails in those early, anxious, conscientious days. I was prepared to worship fly-fishing with a pure, exclusive devotion and leave the worms behind. I supposed that true angling aristocrats would be puzzled by the mention of worms in connection with fishing. But Tom swore that he would have nothing to do with flies. He had been brought up on worms; he had always had worms; he regarded flies as immoral and probably ineffective. Why should a trout bite at a bit of tinfoil and rag? He had as a boy caught scores of trout on a fishhook—there seemed to be some sturdy republican virtue about calling a hook a fishhook—on a fishhook baited with starved little wormlets dug up in barren lands. With these leviathans, daintily and boastfully labelled "Cultivated Dew-Worms," as if to hint at some sort of Academy for selected worms of good family, he made no doubt of being followed by the fishes up the trees. In fact, his frugal soul suggested fifty worms, each of which could be partitioned into four, giving him two hundred potential baits, since I should be sticking to flies. However, as I said, we took one hundred.

Naturally, Tom had no comments on the flies, though he seemed fascinated by the brilliant plumage of some, and would, I believe, have risen to a Montreal. When I bought wet flies, he did ask me, I think quite innocently, what had determined me to choose them instead of dry ones. The question was as awkward as the choice had been. I could not remember that Jim had ever said anything about moisture or the lack of it in connection with flies, and I had never before bought any of my own. I had used Jim's old ones—and worms. Off-hand, I should have ignorantly sworn that Jim's flies were dry when bought, but when I saw both kinds before me in the show-case, I realized that my basis of judgment was worthless, for both wet and dry flies seemed equally dry. Consequently, when I perceived that there were at least these two kinds of flies, and that I should have to choose between them, I was embarrassed. If there is anything I do hate to appear to be, it is *new*. A *new* fly-fisherman! I felt like a bridegroom. Somehow or other, I am not sure how, for the confusion of that moment is blurred now, but by some means short of honest asking, I found out which I was supposed to buy, and bought. Sometimes I have doubts as to how far I deceived the salesman, who is very tactful; sometimes I have no doubts at all. I did not answer Tom's question for a moment, until a helpful clamour of sound arose at the door. Then I mumbled the first two lines of *The Burial of Sir John Moore*, which must have satisfied his curiosity, for he said nothing further. I have always since then intended to learn the difference between dry and wet flies, partly to satisfy an avid thirst for general knowledge, partly because Tom might some day remember that he did not hear the answer to his question.

In reels, lines and hooks—we selected hooks far too large of course, No. 6—and a cheap casting-rod, and a landing-net, and swivels and things, Tom showed a much more lively interest. We bought the troll lure that was reported by returning anglers to make the only sure appeal to trout in the northern lakes that summer, a fancy new contraption the name of which I have forgotten.

As for our grocery and meat shopping, I shall content myself with that simple summary, the Grub List, and let its eloquence suffice. It is as follows, as I copy it from the original, still tenderly preserved among the archives, together with the comments appended after the trip:

Bacon, 7 lbs. (None too much, even with good fishing.)
Chipped Beef, ½ lb.
Klim, 2 pound cans.
Evaporated Milk, 6 small cans. (Used only two.)
Sugar, 4 lbs. (More than enough.)
Onions, 12 large Spanish.
Cheese, 1 lb.
Oranges, 6.

OUR SETTING OUT

Salt, 1 lb. (Plenty.)
Rolled Oats, 6 lbs. (5 would have been plenty.)
Butter, 4 lbs.
Tea, 1 lb.
G. Washington coffee, 1 can. (We were staunchly British, and coffee was almost all brought back.)
Prunes, 3 lbs.
Beans, 2 lbs.
Jam, Strawberry, 1 lb.
Pancake flour, 4 packages.
Chocolate bars, 7 ten-cent ones.
Bread, 9 loaves.

I may say that the total cost of the grub proper was eleven dollars and sixty-three cents, and that it was expected to last for about sixteen days.

Blankets we had, two pairs. One was warm, adequately long, grey, made by some decent nondescript firm of common people. The other had been shortened and narrowed by many washings, some non-professional; to eke out its scantiness, a piece of discarded blanket of muddy white colour and totally unrelated fabric had been sewn on one end of it. Tom is smaller than I. Obviously, this second blanket should have been his, but the thought of letting him sleep in it did not even require to be dismissed, because it never came to me. For this blanket is a red one, with three—alas! not four—significant black lines on one edge, lines which, with magnificent contempt for lexicographers, are called points. Know all men that my red blanket has been woven for me these three hundred years and more by the Company of Gentlemen Adventurers Trading into Hudson's Bay. When I roll myself into it, I am a bearded factor, pulling that blanket out of a bale at York Factory, and selling it dourly to my feathered, silent, stately Cree self for too many beaver skins, trapped along the bitter reaches of the North Saskatchewan.

Our tent calls for little comment. It shows traces of mildew, and leaks quite a while at one of the seams, even though at the time of this trip it was fairly new. It would be despised by the heroic as too commodious, for it is seven by seven, with a two-foot wall. The heroic tent must have no wall, and does not completely close. On the other hand ours is not a sybaritic tent. This latter has a canvas floor and an outer tent and a portico. I have dreamt that I dwelt in silken tents, but awakened always to canvas.

The Canoe! Ah! herein I am more affluent than the Sportsman of vast equipment. He does not own his canoe, for a canoe is an integral part of a guide, and is indentured with him. My canoe, over twenty years old, is mine own. During fifty weeks of the year it takes up room begrudged in our small cellar, and accumulates dust. It interferes with every possible cellar activity by reason of its sixteen feet of length, and its general intractability of shape. It is slung from the ceiling along the only roomy compartment, and makes of that a menace to life and a guarantee of deep damnation. In short, it is a nuisance to society.

At present it is green. Originally it was grey, and when the proper time came to paint it again—or rather three years after that time—I flirted with red. It seemed to me that all painted canoes in poetry were red. You know. . . . *The slim red shape vanished noiselessly into the mist*, or round the bend or over the falls. I do not remember why my canoe was not painted red at that time. Possibly the Sale did not include red paint. I shall always regret that lost opportunity. Now I am too old and fat for red, and am condemned to green for ever, unless perhaps there should some day be an irresistible Sale of Red Canoe Paint.

OUR SETTING OUT

It is canvas-covered. The Hero has of course his Birch-bark. I have several times paddled a birch-bark canoe. Once I paddled one alone across a fair-sized lake, and back again. The back again was because there was no road by which to walk back and carry the thing. I am glad I did paddle that canoe. Now, when a Hero speaks, I sometimes venture to remark that a birch-bark is fine for the portage, but a bit cranky, especially if one is alone. The Hero must naturally express surprise that anybody should find it cranky. He uses it constantly himself, likes the feel of it somehow. But he always treats me for a time with new respect. My own canoe, however, is solid burgess type, broad-bottomed, wide-waisted, with a mighty keel. It has most of the vulgar, prosaic safeness of a scow. It weighs about seventy pounds. It is not graceless. No canoe, not even the most painstakingly family one, can be anything but enchantingly beautiful. It bears honourable scars. There are certain historic scratches. On the left side, bow-wards, is its pride, a clumsy, irregular, extensive lump, like part of a relief map of Palestine or Sparta. That is a patch. On one golden autumn day, while the canoe was still young, as we paddled gaily along to the pace of *En roulant ma boule roulant*, a rasp-like rock rose up and tore a deathly strip of canvas from the frame of my hitherto unmarred treasure. I mended it thoroughly, but not neatly. On one of the thwarts is the piece of rope knotted to receive the blades of the paddles on the portage. When the canoe was making ready for her maiden voyage, that rope was knotted by as true a son of the Canadian woods as ever trod them, albeit his youth was spent in Derbyshire. It has never been removed. Then there is an extra thwart which Tom put in, for greater ease in portaging. As for paddles, we had two, tried and therefore trusted. We were advised to take three, but we had an infantile confidence in our ability to avoid accidents, and declined the extra weight.

My chief difficulty with the Canoe has been a name. When it was new, it seemed to need no name. *The Canoe* or *She* was amply thrilling. Later on, during the years when the duty of re-painting weighed heavily upon me, though not heavily enough, I pondered over a name. This name, once found, was to be painted upon it, in plain white characters. But when I finally decided upon *Goulais*, rather than *Algoma*, the name froze on my brush. A name on a canoe, however severely painted, was too unheroic, smacked too much of cushion-burdened, gramophone-bearing, lovey-dovey craft that lolled up and down the swooning lagoons of towns and cities. Nevertheless, in the privacy of camp or lake or river, I would sometimes call her the *Goulais*. But even to this day a shyness comes over me when I try to give the Canoe a name. I thought that I might use the name in the comparative remoteness of this narrative, like a bashful lover who can wax bold by way of the postal service, though he be stricken dumb in the presence. It's no use: it can't be helped; she can only be the Canoe. A third name has been suggested by two friends, but it lacks respect, romance, bushiness, appropriateness, and even intelligibility to any but the college songsters of a generation or two ago and a few girl guides. I give it out of a burdensome necessity laid upon me for completeness. It is *The Walloping Window-Blind*.

There were various other sundries in our outfit, but for the moment, and indeed until they come into the story, they will be dismissed as the Etceteras. They included two cans of soup. By this time I had learned the folly of liquid supplies, which merely add weight of water. Two pounds of white beans will supply a dozen meals, whereas two pounds of canned beans contribute only to two meals, and bush water, boiled, is quite as nourishing, and fully as healthful, as canning-factory water. But there are usually one or two meals before the portaging begins; hence, before the need of economy in weight requires consideration. The soup was for these. Even portability can be so completely disregarded for the first meal that we set out with a large, juicy blueberry pie.

One superfluity is regularly taken along with us. I have a modest camera. At one time I bought a book on the rudiments of amateur photography, and a technical manual with a fancy dial to show the actinic values of the several hours, weeks and months of the year, together with instructions as to proper exposures. These aids to perfection must still be somewhere about the place. At an indefinitely future time I shall resume the study of photography, but not so long as I can continue to find delight on stormy February evenings in poring over my botched camera records of bygone fishing joys. Until then I expose my lens one twenty-fifth of a second, and restrict my experiments to deciding between eleven and sixteen for aperture. This should convey enough information as to my standing in the subject of photography.

As I say, I have a camera. Now I maintain that one camera for every two inhabitants is adequate for Canada. It is a silly idea for Tom to carry a camera into the bush when I have one. His does take better pictures than mine, but why have two? Tom's camera has served one useful purpose, I must admit. He is an enthusiastic trail man, and at that time was an inexperienced one. Now it seemed at times advisable to husband my strength—naturally for the good of the expedition as a whole, including Tom. Unfortunately, the only way of husbanding one's strength in such a case is by unhusbanding the other man's. Sometimes, as I watched with solicitude the piling up of Tom's load on his bowed shoulders, and hunched my own appraisingly, conscience awoke and tapped me timidly. Then I would mutter very low, "Well, you would bring that kodak of yours along. It's your own fault if you have to carry an extra twenty pounds!" Thereupon conscience would mumble drowsily, turn over once, and slumber dreamlessly again. On the whole, I am glad that Tom brings his camera.

Probably there are items which I have not mentioned, and which occur to the mind of the reader. More likely there are many items which the reader did not require to have mentioned. In compensation, I shall omit all further description of our preparations, shall load the canoe silently on top of the car, shall say nothing of adventures between Toronto and North Bay, nothing of the irksome wait for the Transcontinental Limited which took our disreputable but clean persons and belongings on board at eleven o'clock that night, before plunging into the wilderness of northern Algonquin Park. I shall say even less of the miserable efforts to sleep, and shall resume the narrative only at the point where a facetious trainman shook us awake and shouted, "Next town, Radiant!" We gathered our stuff, and when the train came to a stop in the inky blackness of two o'clock on a moonless, cloudy summer night, we tumbled into the opaqueness. We followed the trainman's lantern up to the baggage-coach, from which our canoe was being unloaded.

"Good night! Good luck!"

The lantern swung its signal, the trainman climbed aboard; in another minute the rear lights of the Limited had disappeared round the bend; and the blackness settled upon us. We were in the bush.

PACK AND PADDLE

CHAPTER II

THE CHILLINESS had roused us, but for a minute or two after the train had disappeared and the sound had ceased to buzz along the rails, we stood by our stuff in silence and breathed in the remoteness. Then, from its place at the top of my little haversack, I pulled out our trusty flashlight, newly equipped with batteries, and sent a pathetic beam along the platform in the general direction of the station. Each of us shouldered a piece of dunnage. While we despise the works of men, we intended to sleep in the station during the few remaining hours of that night. The station might be about twenty feet by eight, and it is divided into two non-communicating parts, each supplied with an outside door. The smaller part has no window, and the door has always been locked whenever I have been there, for which reason its contents remain a mystery. The other part is never locked. It has two small windows, benches along one end and part of two sides, a stove and a supply of wood. Anyone reaching Radiant at two o'clock in the morning is expected to be a guest of the railway in the little station on the night of arrival.

We opened the door, and immediately fell back in disorder. Outside, at that time of night, the mosquitoes were quiescent, but inside they were instantly and extensively active. Accordingly, we had to bring up the rest of our stuff and undo every bag to find our mosquito-quelling Flytox, which should of course have been at the top of my little haversack, along with the flashlight. By the smoky light of a lantern which I neglected to mention as part also of the furnishings in our hospice, we finally found the Flytox. (At this point I abandon the capital letter. Flytox may be a trade name, and we may be advertising a commercial product, and there may be, and I presume are, quite as good moppers-up of black flies and mosquitoes as this preparation, but we had been led to it, and knew no other. It was good for Job and Daniel, and 'twas good enough for us.) During the process of finding the flytox and attaching the sprayer to the container, we were devoured. We could not remember where we had put the fly-repellent, known hereinafter as *fly-dope*, which was to be applied to our persons, and which ought to have been immediately available at the top of my little haversack. Finally we flytoxed the place, and a great peace descended upon it. The peace could be maintained only by keeping the room hermetically sealed, but at the time we could see only good in such sealing. We spread the tent out on the floor as a mattress, disposed our individual blankets, and turned in. And over! I have slept on asphalt and cement pavements; I have slumbered soundly on freshly rolled, still warm steel rails; I have snored stentoriously on undulating roots and pyramidical stones; and I swear that all these are as down when compared with the unyielding flatness of a common wooden floor. It is the most unaccommodating substance known; it yields not itself to the contours of the human form, nor does it permit that form to yield to it. Every one of my bones was between forty and fifty years old, and every one roared aloud that dreadful night. Still, I must have slept, for there came a time when I was conscious of early daylight, somewhat suddenly.

I put on my shoes—all I had removed—and slipped out to be sure that the canoe was safe. The town of Radiant, as the merry trainman had called it, lay before me, and all that mighty heart was lying still. The inhabitants of Radiant consist—or at that time consisted—of a Park Ranger, a Fire Ranger, five sectionmen, two wives, one sister-in-law, and three children. The buildings are such as are proper for the housing and occupation of the inhabitants, but comprise in addition some dozen or so log buildings belonging to a lumber company which operates in these regions during certain winter seasons. The town climbs up gently from a lake now marked on the map as Radiant, but then known as Trout. I know quite well that we have six or seven hundred Trout Lakes in the Province of Ontario, and only one Radiant Lake. Nevertheless, I feel a definite resentment at the change, and decline to accept it. These things should be left as Adam named them.

By the time I had come back to the station, Tom was awake. We made our breakfast on the stove, then hunted up the Park Ranger to secure the various permits necessary, that is, our travel permits and our angling licenses. I wanted Tom to meet the Park Ranger, and I had hoped the Fire Ranger as well would be there. The latter was away, but in subsequent years Tom came to anticipate meeting both of them again with as much eagerness as I did myself. Blessings on ye, Messrs. Nadon and Proulx, our blessing and the big bannock too! The former of you taught us, not once nor twice, that officials were human beings and not a separate species, that an official could be both obliging and faithful, both genial and honest, both courteous and efficient. Almost any other official in the Park would have taught us the same lesson, but we happened to learn it from you. The second of you, in your appropriated loggers' shanty, over mighty helpings of ravishing pea-soup from the great black cauldron bubbling on the stove, helpings thrice renewed and still urged, eaten with the sister-in-law's home-baked bread, and with tea strong enough to climb its own steep—the second of you, I say, with your tales of the perfect lumber-camp, your teamster's pride in the horses you used to drive for Gillespie, your joy in deer and bear and wolves, with your speech that rang like the sound of the cross-cut saw at twenty below, emphatic as the blows of your own bright axe in the morning, colourful as the gay Assumption belt you used to wear—the second of you made us realize that the race of natural lumberjacks had not yet died out.

In your camp, too, I heard Ed tell some of his authentic experiences when he worked for the great Paul Bunyan. I have no idea who Ed was, or why he was in your camp that night. It was the year before this trip of Tom's and mine, and I was coming out with Jim. We intended to wait in the dreary station for the midnight train, due at one-thirty, but you invited us to sit beside your hospitable fire. We found Ed already there. I do not recall how he was induced to talk. When memory picks up the wave-length, he is already speaking, and this is an approximation to what he is saying.

"Talkin' about jams, Frenchy, I mind me of one jam that was a humdinger. It was in the square-timber days, and course I was workin' for old Paul. I wasn't a hewer or anythin'. All I done was some of the scorin'. Paul was cuttin' up along Georgian Bay that winter, an' he got a contract for a lot of round logs for masts or flagpoles or somethin'. This was the first time they ever sent logs out in the round and kinda loose. Before that they always rafted 'em. Paul started to raft them round logs together just like he been used to, but then he got the idea of just lettin' 'em go and follerin' 'em down and that's what they all been doin' ever sence.

"So we brung them logs down Lake Huron and Lake Erie till we got in the Niagara River. She was runnin' hell bent for leather. That was the spring after the Winter of the Blue Snow. You remember, Frenchy, what an awful slew of indigo blue water there was tryin' to get away that spring. Old man Reckitts made a hell of a lot of money out of that Blue Snow. He compressed it, and they been sellin' it ever sence for bluein' clothes.

"Well, the Niagara was chock full of this damn indigo blue snow-water, when along comes us with the drive. There was one place along there where there was a kind of swift water, a kind of drop, maybe ten or twelve feet, and around a bend. They'd been so much snow that winter that there'd been a couple of bad landslides nigh this bend and a lot of trees and stuff was layin' out there makin' a kind of island. Well, sir, them logs begun to catch at them two landslides, and before you could skin an eyeball we had two as pretty jams as you ever laid eyes on. The one below wasn't so bad, and Paul set the gang to work clearin' it away.

"But this here upper one—about half a mile above where the gang was workin'—she was a daisy. I was comin' along with Babe—that's Paul's blue ox I was tellin' you about—and I watched her pile up. Them logs 'd come asizzlin' along and then they'd strike her kerboom. You'd see a two-hundred footer hit her—and then it'd go up maybe a quarter of a mile straight up in the air and come down kersmash and help pile up the tangle.

"Just to show you how fast she piled up. When I seen her start, I says to myself, 'Well, we're damn well here for a couple of weeks before we break this jam, so I might as well light up the old corn-cob.' Babe was standin' there, brushin' logs off with his tail that was fallin' all around us. I guess he thought the flies was bad for so early. Well, I took a look first at the jam. She was piled up maybe half a mile high. Then I takes enough time off to fill my pipe, and then I looks again before I lights her.

"Well, I know it's kinda hard to believe, but in that time, and it can't have been more than half an hour—we was workin' by the hour on the drive, and not by the piece, so it took longer to fill a pipe or anything like that—well, in that time she'd piled up so's I couldn't see the top. There was a cloud had got caught part way up it too.

"About this time up comes Paul.

" 'Ed,' he says, 'she's a nasty mess.'

" 'She sure is,' I says. 'How far back is she jammed, do you s'pose?'

" 'Well, she was piled up about twenty miles back, when I come away about ten minutes ago,' says Paul. 'I paced it as I came along. She's solid that far back with logs, and the river's pilin' up all over the country.'

"I could see there wasn't hardly any comin' through; water, I mean.

" 'See that bunch of logs stickin' out?' says Paul.

"There was one place about in the middle where there was a big mess of logs bulgin' out about a quarter of a mile out of the main jam.

" 'Well,' says Paul, 'I got a notion that there bulge is bunched around the key log. She's too hard to get at with the peavy, and she's too risky anyhow. I'm goin' to hitch Babe to that mess and give it a jolt. We'll just let Babe stay right here and fetch her slonchways from the side. I'll hook the big skiddin' chain around that mess, and then I'll pass the chain up to you. When I say go, you let Babe give it hell.'

" 'But where'll you be?' I says.

" 'I ain't goin' to be in front of them logs,' Paul says, and he kinda grins.

"Well, pretty soon here was me and Babe standin' by the shore, so close Babe's tail was hangin' over kinda. There was Paul foolin' around with his peavy, workin' a place to fit the chain. He seemed to find it sort of hard. He'd pull out half a dozen logs and throw 'em to one side. But most of them logs was over two hundred foot long, and they was clumsy to work with.

"All of a sudden I went kinda sick. You know that low sort of quiet crackin' splittin' sound a jam makes when she's givin' 'way, Frenchy. I heard it, and I seen the bulge movin' just a leetle, and then I seen a three-hundred-foot log shoot up in the air, like it'd been squeezed out of some kinda paste tube or somethin'. I knowed Paul'd loosened the key log. I tried to yell, but I couldn't, and my blood froze that hard it took four days and a half to thaw me out afterwards.

"I seen Paul jerk his peavy out and turn around and look down the river. I'd forgot all about them men down below, right in the way of that tremendjous jam and her a-movin'. Well, sir, Paul let one beller out of him, and then he shoved his back against that bulge of logs, and braced his feet on the rock bottom of the river. I could see the men makin' tracks for the shore. Paul was breathin' so hard he was sendin' up steam enough to make a kind of mist. That mist is floatin' around there yet, a lot of it.

"Then I seen Paul beginnin' to sink. I couldn't do a thing but gawp, but one of my eyes popped right out. Did you notice that left eye lookin' kind of funny? That's the one. Ole the Blacksmith shoved her right back in with the little tongs, but she never went the same again. Just then it was kind of a good thing. I could stand there and watch the men runnin' for the shore and Paul sinkin' down all at the same time. First off I couldn't tell what was happenin' and then I seen what it was. He was holdin' so hard agin that jam he was pushin' the river-bed down. By this time the gang below was all safe on shore and I yells to Paul. And it wasn't any too soon neither. I begun to hear that there crackin' agin. I thought maybe Paul's strength was givin' 'way, but I'd ought to of knowed better, only I was kind of silly with all the strain and everything. Then I seen what it was. Paul'd sank so far he was losin' his purchase on the logs. The logs was gettin' throwed up and fallin' all around me and Babe again. I was kind of standin' under Babe's belly; that's how they wasn't hittin' me. And Babe was switchin' his tail to knock 'em off, thinkin' they was flies.

"It's a lucky thing maybe he was, too. Paul might of had a nasty time gettin' out, only Babe's tail kind of swung out over the river when he was switchin', and Paul grabbed it and swung like he was on a rope. He kicked agin the jam and that give him a long swing downstream, long enough in fac' so that he lit on shore and knocked down a few trees, but not to hurt. Poor Babe fetched a beller you could've heered forty mile away, and the poor old tail stretched so they had to put a couple of half-hitches in it so it wouldn't drag and get in the way.

"Paul give a kind of a rough estimate he'd sunk down about two hundred and forty feet. Course he pushed the hull bottom of the river down with him. She come back about eighty feet or so when the weight was off her, but she stayed sunk about a hundred and sixty feet or so. And you don't have to take my word for it either, because there she is to this day. Paul had to give up sendin' logs around that way, because this new big falls he made in the Niagara was too rough on 'em. That's a mighty long time ago, Frenchy, but I'm a lot older 'n I look."

By half-past eight, Tom and I were ready for the trail. The first stage was a mile carry along the railway track, to the place where the railway crosses the Petawawa River. Beyond that, the Petawawa would parallel the tracks for some four or five miles—many more, I imagine—but about that distance from the bridge the Crow River, formerly Lavieille Creek, comes tumbling over an old dam into the Petawawa. We follow it up, and away from the railway.

It was not exactly unavoidable, this proceeding down the railway track. Trout Lake, upon which Radiant smiles, is after all merely a bulge in the Petawawa. We could have put the canoe into the water at once and have gone down the river. There were, however, as I told Tom quite truthfully, two or three rapids between the foot of the lake and the railway bridge, and we should have been constantly in and out of the canoe. I was silent as to my real reason. Tom had never been in rapids, except at the Soo, and then as a more or less inactive passenger in a huge canoe under the care of an expert Indian, who was said to dispose of dangerously nervous passengers by means of a primitive method of inducing anaesthesia with a swift and heavy paddle brought down smartly upon the head. Now I was no expert, no Indian; had no paddle to spare, no time, no dexterity in administering anaesthetics: in short, had no faith in the situation at all. I was frankly terrified at the thought of us in the immediate presence of rapids. On that morning, had the possibility presented itself of proceeding along the railway tracks all the way to the fishing grounds, I should have seized upon it with vast relief. Consequently, the mile was welcome, and we proceeded along the tracks.

The term *proceed* sounds somewhat magniloquent to describe the movement of two peaceful, inoffensive men fleeing with their all into the solitude of a semi-northern forest. But anyone who has ever tried travelling by foot along a railroad should understand my difficulty. For reasons that almost anyone can perceive, the great railway engineers have always discouraged walking along their right-of-way, and in fact have made normal walking impossible, by their diabolical spacing of the ties. The pedestrian movement enforced on railroad tracks has seemed to me at times to bear a distinct resemblance to the knight's move in chess. Some dexterous juveniles are able to walk upon the steel rails themselves, but this is of course not practicable for any distance. Hence, quite at a loss for a word to describe accurately and specifically the eccentric and uncomfortable locomotion I am discussing, I have been driven to the indefinite but not actually misleading term *proceeding*. Indeed, as I think about it and remember more clearly the operation, I am struck with the felicity of the expression. A procession often implies, not continuous movement, but occasional and sometimes prolonged pauses. I assure you there were many such.

Most canoe-campers transport everything, I suppose,

in one carry. The Hero is content with so little that he can do this easily. The Sportsman has a guide, whose carrying capacity is always a matter of conjecture, for its limit has never been reached. There is also a breathless young thing who rushes through the woods like wildfire, in shorts, who carries provisions barely sufficient to get him through to the next food depot, and whose boast is in having done in one day what we have dawdled over for a week. But as for us, we have with us the Canoe, enough blanketing and tenting to keep us reasonably warm and dry, all the food required for two and a half weeks, as shown on the Grub List, such other odds and ends as may or may not appear in the chronicle, and Tom's superfluous camera. Moreover, we simply are not heroic. Sorry, but we are not. We must make two trips to get our stuff across a portage.

I presume that a methodical searching into a porous memory would disclose the basis on which our division of loads was made, but at the moment it is a mystery, like the basis of our general distribution of labour on a canoe trip. One or two guiding principles I do recall. The first, which I communicated as a tradition, was that the owner of the canoe should carry it himself. This tradition arose partly from sheer vainglory, and a quite erroneous conviction that I could stand the hardships of the portage better than Tom. I may say that it was modified on the second day out. On short carries it was, and is, jealously observed, but on long ones we began to alternate in carrying the canoe. The second principle is that a man carries his personal sundries, and it may be summed up for us in the responsibility of each man for his own small haversack.

I must add a word—in fact, a paragraph—about the contents of mine, since there are certain family articles which I carry. For instance, there are candle-ends. The flashlight is not to be riotously squandered. It partakes of the character of emergency rations. Its illusory brilliance must be conserved. In the ordinary routine of our camp life, it is used only as the means of illuminating the grand nightly flytoxing. For tent lighting we ordinarily use candles, or rather candle-ends.

Throughout the year, I keep a watchful eye upon candles. Their chief use, in our household, is to convey an impression of a fifteenth century Christmas, and to archaize, if not refine, one or two other rare entertaining occasions. Candles put to such use are partially burned, and after the occasion has passed, I quietly take possession of them and add them to the miscellaneous store in my tackle-box. There are in addition some four or six or eight —they are always in even numbers—which are regarded as ornamental in their own right or are considered necessary to display certain cherished candlesticks. They occupy, in a more or less forgotten manner, permanent positions in the home. As the heats of summer fiercen, these candles gradually assume a gracefully bowed attitude that is not proper to candles. Upon my drawing attention to their incorrect posture, I am usually allowed to appropriate them for my hoard. By the time June comes round, I have a quite large assortment of candle-ends, somewhat more gaudy in colour than is required in the woods, but adequate in candle-power for the trip. It is our proud boast that only once have Tom and I used a regular, full-length, natural-colour candle; and that one we found by a camp-site.

Now from time immemorial the candle-ends belong in my little haversack. So do the blanket-pins, and the flashlight, and the medicine chest, and the cribbage board and cards, and the canoe-mender, and the flytox with its sprayer—and the candlestick, also found one time on a log. I am sure there are other communal articles that go into it, but I cannot at the moment think of any more. I do know, however, that both Tom and I would immediately recognize the proper place for anything I have omitted to mention.

I cannot rid myself of some clinging vestiges of respect for the man who makes one trip on a portage. In an attempt to obtain as large a measure of tolerance as possible from him, I set forth here our impedimenta, itemized as to main containers and comprisers. It is, I promise, my last enumeration. Let me call to mind the stuff as laid out at the beginning of a carry after we have been perhaps two days out. No matter how many times we have gone into the bush together, there is always an element of uncertainty, of raggedness, about the first two carries, wherefore I select a later occasion. Perhaps we are ready to set out on the second lap of the long portage that is broken by camping at the Forks, where the White Partridge joins the Creek.

For us the canoe is not a container, in the sense employed above. Heroes and Guides suspend great weights from thwarts and other suspending places in a canoe carried upside down, but for Tom and me the canoe is load enough. The Pet, a long brown bag, named long ago in bitter irony, falls to Tom's lot. Into it he puts all his clothing, his small pack, and a large part of the food. Usually lying beside it is the tent bundle, very compactly rolled, and enfolding the blankets within its sheltering envelope. Third of the major packs is my own big rucksack. It contains my clothing, my little haversack, and some of the food, chiefly extra cans of powdered milk, and such. In the case of anything which comes in more than one container, the current package goes into an ancient army dunnage bag, carried in the Pet, while the reserves are put into my pack. The bacon, which comes in one vast slab, falls also to my share. Most of the grease areas— I cannot call them spots—on my pack are bacon grease areas. Within the same folds of brown paper which enwrap the bacon nestles the half-pound of chipped beef. I carry the butter pail, and the jam. When everything else is in, the axe, with the handle insinuating its way down the back of the pack, and with its head peeping coyly out of one corner at the top, completes my big load.

In addition, there are impedimenta which are genuine impediments, hideous, misshapen things that must be borne with imprecations and without credit. They do not weigh much; they have no abiding place on shoulder or back; when carried in the hand, they take out of action a sadly needed fly-and-mosquito-fighting force; they are the very devil.

One of these, the least obnoxious, is the coarse grain sack which holds the nine loaves of bread. I must confess to a romantic though waning repugnance against carrying bread into the bush. Bread seems to me to smack too much of the effete life I am fleeing, the life of green vegetables, of the raucous radio, of warm bath-water, of newspapers, of fresh milk, of ties and cuff-links, of refrigeration, of pastry and lectures, of art and social intercourse, of citizenship and womenkind, of cleanliness and white linen sheets, of motor-cars and mattresses. Flour I would take, and as a concession, even pancake flour; and I would scorn the baker as I flipped my flapjack into the air. But Tom adores bread, and watches with unconcealed concern the spread of the green mould through the desiccating loaves. Jim is so insensitive to this exquisiteness of my quivering woodland soul that he does not even stop at bread: he takes eggs!

But no egg shells of ours defile the camp-sites when Tom and I go off a-Juning.

The rough stuff, consisting of the frying-pan and the three billies, is dropped into a sack still coarser in texture than the bread bag. Our billies are covered tin pails, so graduated into small, smaller, smallest, that they form in repose what we might call a nest of billies. The largest is a veritable Pooh-Bah among utensils. For a normal meal it serves first as tea-kettle, next as teapot, then as the kettle for heating dish-water, and finally as the lowly dishpan. The second billy is primarily for cooking porridge, though it may also be used for soaking beans, or prunes, or for mixing pancake batter. In case of need, it may perform all the functions of Billy No. I. Both of these are always swart on the outside, with a fine nap of black velvet adhering not too firmly to them. The third and smallest is never set on the fire. It is the regular soaking-billy. It is also used, if disengaged, for mixing Klim. As the innermost of the three billies in the nest when on the march, it can be kept reasonably clean.

The bag for table service and clean kitchen-ware is always tied to the rough-stuff sack. There are three tin plates, two tin cups, three forks, two knives, three dessert spoons, two table spoons, one long-handled spoon—I believe that we have too many spoons—an egg-beater, dish-mop, dish towel, metal pan-scourer, one bar laundry soap, one long toasting-fork, the prongs of which are continually protruding through the bag and prodding the carrier on the trail. The bag itself is one of four sandbags, the loot of a pillaging expedition one dark afternoon in 1916 in Camp Borden.

We have, too, a gawky bundle, tied up firmly, containing the fishing rods, landing nets, and in these later years the spare paddle. At one time the axe was included, but it was removed because of an annoying suggestion that the bearer of this bundle was an anachronistic lictor, with the fasces. Even though the rods remained, the removal of the axe from that bundle made the lictorial suggestion fairly remote. The remaining hand luggage comprised the tackle-box, which I always carry as a mark of rank, and the box of worms.

Let us say it is a short carry, half a mile, we are making. Tom takes the worms, the two utensil sacks, the bundle with the rods, sometimes the bread bag; I take the canoe. On the second trip, Tom takes the Pet and the tent bundle; I my big pack and the tackle-box, the badge of my seniority.

I should, perhaps, apologize for this long digression. But the fisherman is not smitten with the insensate rigidity of purpose which must look always, thrust always, straight ahead. Fishing is itself a pause for breath. Hence, the fisherman will be tolerant of asides. It may be advisable, however, to remind you that some time ago we set off, or were about to set off, down the railroad track on a mile carry to the bridge over the Petawawa River. Thence we were to paddle and portage some four miles or thereabout, down to where the Creek comes tumbling into a placid, pond-like widening of the river.

I remember the surprising lightness of the canoe as I sauntered off with it on my shoulders, its weight resting easily on my canoe pad. I know that the Hero—or the guide—may knot a sweater round his neck and dispense with any other padding amenities. I do not. Years ago I used to roll my blankets, bandolier-fashion, and rest the canoe on them. There were several disadvantages in this. If the blanket shifted, as it tended to do, it allowed the paddles to do their worst, or it encircled my neck and nearly strangled me. Even if it remained in position, snuggling closely about my neck, it developed within the airless regions of that inverted canoe a steaming heat which I found very trying. Later I had a pad made, on the model of an old one belonging to Jim. It does suggest excess baggage, since it is used for one purpose only, and that thought troubled me occasionally, until the year we met a man carrying a canoe on a wooden yoke. That reconciled me to the pad. He seemed proud of it, and allowed me to lift it and try it on. He gave me its dimensions, and offered me advice as to having it made. He gave me his address, and was most benevolent about it all. It would have been indecent not to be grateful to him. While he was talking to me, and wasting his time in demonstrating his wooden yoke, I was grateful for his interest, just as I am to all those who try to do good to me, to persons like automobile philanthropists, house insulation humanitarians, insurance evangelists, and other similar benefactors. I have been afraid that Tom was somewhat smitten with this contraption, but I may be wronging him. After the Man with the Wooden Yoke had gone on about his other business, we luxuriated in two hours of complete silence.

I am not sure of whether or not Tom helped me up with the canoe. By the second day, even effete I disdain assistance in lifting it up to my shoulders, but often in the aching tenderfootedness of the first day I submit to the friendly offices of the other man in the matter. After about two hundred yards, Tom asked me how it felt. I assured him with conviction that it had never seemed so light, that I had at last, apparently quite by accident, hit upon the correct way of carrying a canoe. The first faint doubtings troubled me immediately thereafter, followed by a growing belief that I had lashed the paddles too closely together, or else not closely enough. A pain in one shoulder admonished me that the canoe was off balance, while a suspicion rose within me that I too must be off balance, to inflict such misery upon myself. I remember the feeling of shamed relief when I decided to stop and readjust the paddles. I tilted the front end of the canoe down, to steady it while I should be taking it off my shoulders, and I stumbled just a little, but enough to send its nose ploughing into the gravel down the grading by the track. I staggered, and Tom called to me to wait and he would help me with it, and I did wait hours while he ran twenty feet, and we got it down, and my shoes were filled with gravel, and I wished that Tom would break a leg and end the trip.

My method of picking up a canoe is highly improper and inefficient, but I am one of the old dogs that cannot be taught new tricks, and learn the old ones badly. As I was taught, the two paddles are laid across two of the thwarts, lengthwise of the canoe, and lashed into place there, far enough apart to rest on the shoulders, quite close to the neck. After the paddles have been lashed in place, the carrier takes hold of the two sides by the gunwale, near the stern, and turns the canoe over as he raises the stern over his head, allowing the nose to remain braced against the ground. He then moves forward until he reaches the point of balance. He has inserted his head between the lashed paddles, and when finally he lifts the whole craft from the ground, it balances upon his shoulders. The properly trained man will, I understand, first dandle the canoe upon his knee, and thence lift it in one easy swing to position.

The real canoe-man takes much of the weight on a tump-line, I am told, but I do not. Occasionally I will relieve the shoulders for a time by allowing the weight to come on my head, but I do it in a very unskilful and despicable manner which commands no one's respect, not even Tom's. When I am carrying my canoe on the trail, the nose tilts slightly downward, with the disquieting result that I cannot see anything above, or more than a few feet beyond me, unless I deliberately shift the balance. As I mentioned earlier, the rear lashings are permanent. The blades of the paddles, which should, I believe, be at the front, but are not, are thrust through knotted loops. These loops have grown rather loose with the lapse and the use of twenty years, and with the succession of paddles for which they were not originally fitted, but their knottings are sacred. They were knotted by Samivel. We depend on the front lashing, done with the long painter, to keep the paddles firmly in place.

When I first owned the canoe, I was very proud of the distance between the middle and bow thwarts. It created immense cargo space, and caused envy among my friends. But it was unsatisfactory for carrying. When the paddles were lashed on, the carrying part of them was too long, and the resultant spring increased the difficulty of portaging the canoe. That is why Tom made our one structural alteration, putting in the extra thwart.

We rested, and shifted loads, and jested bitterly, and cursed the liar who had assured us that the bridge was only a mile away, and emptied our shoes, and went on and on. Finally, to our amazement, we actually did see the bridge. A delightful breeze was coming down the gorge of the Petawawa, and the rapids roared below us. We listened for trains, although we understood that there would be none for two days. Still, some two hundred yards of narrow bridge dictated caution, and while we could be sure that in the easy escapability of the regular land right-of-way there would be no train to trouble us, life had mocked us both so often that we unconsciously considered it capable of materializing a train at any moment to entrap us on that slender thread of bridge. The railroad ties were evenly and closely spaced, but the pleasant breeze swung the canoe disconcertingly about my head, with the faintest of suggestions to an alert imagination that I might lose my balance and be toppled over into the lively commotion a hundred odd feet below. Then the roaring receded, and the ground came up to reassure us, and the bridge became a culvert and a high track. After another hundred yards we saw the first of those beloved comforters, the fire rangers' signs.

These are of heavy cardboard, black on a bright yellow ground, and are designed primarily to admonish campers as to the danger of fire. The most spectacular contains a huge black hand with fingers outspread and pointing upward, and an invitation to stop and consider whether you have extinguished your camp-fire before leaving it. I may say that, to the best of my belief, we have. A profound psychologist, employed at some time by some department somewhere, hit on the device of using these signs to mark the beginnings of portages and the terminations thereof. Consequently, campers go about lakes seeking a sign, and meditate perforce on their quenching duties each time they find one. The signs must be frequently replaced, because, if the rangers are to be believed, as of course all rangers are, Bruin has a tendency to go berserk at the sight of the signs and tear them down, if he can.

We ploughed down the gravel of the track grading, and out upon the richness of a genuine though miniature trail. The quality of remoteness in space differs from that of remoteness in time, and I know of nothing that illustrates this better than a trail. The roar of humanity, dulled through remoteness in space, is still raucous with pain and menace and cultivated lusts, but the poignancy in the low murmur of the remote in time has lost the tones of pain and menace. Temporal continuity is as inescapable as spatial continuity, and indeed the chain of being through time is more readily recognized than the vast enmeshing of the continuum in space, but the mind of man requires very little aid to set up its little partition between the present and the past. On the trail, a gentle shower, effacing the sharp outline of a boot-sole in the mud; a single leaf, fallen carelessly across a track; the tiny, patient erosions of two quiet days—any of these will create the illusion of infinite remoteness between the man on the trail and his predecessor. That illusion once set up, he revels in the silent communion with all who have gone before, in the concave path, the healed-over blaze, the entroughed leaves, the brown powdered punk, even in the dim places where the foot feels the trail rather than the eye sees it.

We passed joyously along this trail and through an open camp-site to the water's edge. Beside the river, here peaceful and sedgy after the turmoil of the rapids, we sank on the ground by our discharged loads and looked rapturously at each other. The trip was about to begin. On the railroad we had had no sense of being in the bush, no ecstasy. Although we had seen nobody along the track, we had still been hearing the hideous clangour of humanity. We were not yet away from the railroad, for it ran parallel to the river for the first five miles of our course, if one may call two lines parallel which occasionally come into sight of each other. Moreover, we had to go back over that track for the rest of our stuff. Even so, this was one of the special moments of the trip. Another would be at this same spot, when we should push off from shore. There would be still others, to be duly solemnized at the proper time.

Tom rolled a cigarette; I filled my pipe. A chipmunk scampered across the path we had just come down. We gazed at it with adoration. Now we were among our own kin. I saw it as the striped jester prancing ahead of our pre-Cambrian procession of moose, mice, martens and mink; of beavers and bears; of ducks and deer; of woodchucks and weasels and wolves; of loons and lynxes; of rabbits and (w)rens; of porcupines and partridges; of squirrels and skunks; of whip-poor-wills and whisky-jacks; of owls and owlets. (I am very sorry about those owlets, but I couldn't leave a blank file, nor could I for some reason comfortably associate an owl with an otter.) We are very childish about chipmunks, Tom and I.

But there was not much time for loitering. We pretended that we should be content for this day to reach the Creek, that we should not try to make the fishing spots until the morrow. In reality, I had set my heart on trying for trout at the Forks in the gathering dusk of that selfsame day. I could see us standing on the old black apron of the abandoned chute, casting into the dark waters, facing into the sunset across the opening in the valley, shouting to each other to get the landing net and help with this monster, and finally desisting from sheer satiety. So, after five minutes, we trudged back along the railroad, and the way seemed longer than when we had been carrying loads. Already habits were being formed, however, and our second trip was very matter-of-fact, very uneventful, almost efficient.

We loaded the canoe. In the bow, the rough stuff and the dishes, and the bundle of rods. Between Tom and me, the Pet, the tent, my pack; on top of them the bread.

Under my seat and in the stern behind me, the tackle-box and the worms, the axe, and the butter pail. Tom climbed over the stuff to his seat in the bow. I shoved the canoe off and crawled over the stern. We thrust the paddles against the sand and pushed. Slowly, half-poled, half-paddled, the canoe swished its way out through the reeds. Tom gave a little lurch. His paddle had not touched bottom when he had expected it to do so. We were off.

I suppose that no more self-contained feeling is possible to man than comes to the canoeing camper at this moment. Gathered about him within a space of somewhat less than thirty square feet are his transportation, his shelter and warmth, his complete wardrobe, all his food except that which he hopes to catch, his implements of the chase, his hospital, his entertainment, his social and political institutions, indeed the whole of society except women. If he has shopped wisely, he is as completely equipped with necessities as ever was Robinson Crusoe. He has no cares, for he has all he needs, and little else. His ambitions are modest, and all but one are likely to be attained. He will not, of course, achieve his supreme ambition, that of catching on a light line, with his favourite fly, a trout at least a pound bigger than any of his friends or acquaintances has caught. Tom and I at any rate cannot achieve that ambition, though we share it, for they do not grow in our particular streams, these giants. We hope only to catch a bigger one than we ourselves have hitherto taken.

We paddled twelve minutes, and reached the first of the five rapids on our stretch of the Petawawa. A shaggy riverman one day told me the names of all these, names redolent of log-drivers and bateaux, and I noted them all carefully on a piece of bacon-wrapping paper long since lost. The first two were merely short stretches of swift water which even I was prepared to run. Now Tom's education had to begin in earnest. Destiny, working largely through a predisposition to fat, has thrust upon me from time to time responsibilities for which I was totally unfitted. In any canoe trip that I have taken I have weighed so much more than my companion that I have of necessity been given the stern place, the position of responsibility. As one consequence, I have never learned the craft of bow-man. But I do know that to him falls the look-out job, so far as imminent rocks are concerned, and that he must often fend the canoe away from these perils with light, delicate thrusts. Jim can do it with the grace of a sculptured Greek athlete, and with an accuracy that removes all anxiety. I explained to Tom as well as I could what I thought was Jim's technique. I told him the little I knew about submerged rocks. I told him more than I knew about the meanings of ripples, about the breakings that indicated rocks too close to the surface for safety. I held forth on the significance of colour in relation to rocks in water. I enlarged upon the upsetting and lacerating properties of rocks. All this I did in the twelve minutes of paddling before we reached the first fast water. I did a thorough job. From one or two disturbing experiences of earlier years I had developed a fear of rocks lurking just below the surface of canoeing waters, and I think I was quite earnest about the subject.

If communication of the artist's emotion be of the essence of great art, then I am, or at any rate was at that time, a great artist. For I undoubtedly communicated an emotion with respect to rocks. Tom developed during twelve and a quarter minutes—twelve minutes of paddling and a quarter-minute of scooting—a horror of rocks which is the nearest approach to monomania that I have observed in my immediate circle. We may be in the middle of a lake, with two hundred feet of water under us, but if there is the slightest sudden wind-ripple, Tom gets all in a dither, and swears that the water shoals hereabouts. On this same lake, with a wind howling around us, and queer-shaped masses of cloud being hurled across a tortured sky, and breaking foam preceding green sheets of water that slither in over the gunwale, and torn-up, twisty waves that leave the paddle pawing helplessly in the air; when I am sweating in an agony of terror, or numb with a sense of impending widowhood thrust upon an untrusting female; when I am calculating with despair the enormous distance from the nearest shore, and realizing the impossibility of cutting across to the nearest shore in any event, with the wind as it is—while I am doing these things, Tom sings high in the gale, and throws out great bravoes, and says ha! ha! among the trumpeting tempests, and in general acts like an idiot in a holocaust. But on a stream, with water varying in depth from three and a half feet to minus two feet, with the shore three or four yards away, with or without a slight speeding up of the current, Tom cowers and rages.

There will probably come no more fitting time to describe our badges of servitude than now. A brief moment ago, in describing Tom's reactions to a storm at lake, I suggested that I have a wife. She is convinced that I shall be drowned unfailingly. I think that it is not so much my being drowned that she finds distasteful, as my being uselessly drowned in the prosecution of selfish pleasures, and away from home. Accordingly, my departure on a fishing trip was wont in former times to resemble the setting-forth on his last criminal exploit of a callous and brutal gunman, leaving a faithful, God-fearing spouse, with an active endowment of the second sight.

This was in former times. Some few years ago, and

before the trip of which this is a chronicle, an increasing sense of guilt compelled me to a desperate measure of humiliation. It appears that among the sensible precautions taken by some deep-water sailors of small craft is the occasional wearing of a kapok life-jacket. In an evil moment I volunteered to wear one of those things if the domestic objections to a proposed expedition were withdrawn. Since that time I have been held up to private ridicule frequently, to public scorn and in the presence of a noble fellowship of anglers once, and to secret contempt I know not how often. You may bet your uttermost dollar that Tom has to wear one—I saw to that. Partly, of course, for his own safety.

For neither Tom nor I can swim. Because of this, almost all our friends shake their heads, and warn us that we should not be found in any such cranky vehicle as a canoe. They are quite right. Never venture into a canoe unless you can swim well. If you do, above two or three times, and have not yet been drowned, you will become so enamoured of canoeing that no amount of prudent counsel or sensible reflection will drive out of your head the fantastic notion that you will not fall out of your canoe. Sooner or later you will fall out, and you can only pray that the kindly Providence which our honest forefathers deemed to have special care over silly folk may cause you to be dumped in drenching but not dangerous places. Neither Tom nor I should ever go a-paddling, tra la la!

I promised that I would wear that jacket whenever I should be in the canoe. I wore it with horror and shame the first trip after I bought it. I skulked behind the wifely petticoat and waved its protecting folds at Jim. I emphasized my hen-pecked condition, and exalted my honour as a man of my word in wearing the jacket under all circumstances. In the secret of my reins I soon was mightily holpen. For I had always been troubled with an inner shuddering at our setting forth over any extensive water, when I considered, as I invariably did, that a misadventure was likely to have only one end for me, and also that in these latter days, with the decay of faith and what not, the fool seemed to have little better protection against his folly than the wise man against his.

We approached the first of the two bits of swift water.

"Hadn't we better land now?" Tom asked, without turning round.

"Land? What for?"

"Well, hey! you're not going to run that big cataract, are you?"

"Sure! You watch for rocks and we'll be down in no time."

'We're on one now!" Tom cried, as he lunged frantically at a rock some fifteen feet away, nearly overturning the canoe.

"Damn you! Keep quiet!" I bellowed.

Tom yelled again and plunged his paddle straight down into the water on the other side, and pushed at a rock we had passed before his paddle touched the water. There was a grinding sound, the bow of the canoe stopped, was lifted, hung. The stern was pulled swiftly around. I prised against the gunwale with my paddle to save the craft from going broadside down the stream. Now, the danger real and known, Tom acted, quickly and surely. The canoe was not heavily caught. The slight, accurate push against the rock raised it free and gave it enough side thrust to straighten the course. Before we fully realized that we were clear of our obstruction, we had shot out into the eddy at the foot of the swift and were already slowing up.

"Fine!" I said encouragingly. "That's your first rapid, and all's well. Let's light up."

Tom grunted, took in his paddle and pulled out his pipe. He did not turn to look at the mildly tumbling waters we had just come through. I knew that his feelings had been hurt. He is not accustomed to being sworn at with impunity.

Our pipes lighted, we paddled on, but not for long. Four or five minutes, no more, and we could hear the pleasant murmur that told of another somewhat abrupt change of level. A half bend in the river, and there it was, very similar to the first, though slightly longer. Tom turned and glared at me.

"You're not going to run this?" he said.

There was nothing I could think of that I wanted to do less than to run that stretch. But I could see Jim coolly preparing to enjoy a little respite from the labour of paddling. I could see other parties lightly shooting down. I could see the voyageurs relaxing, and probably spitting *tabac canadien* in derision at such puny water. I could see birch-barks, guided by quiet Indians, bobbing nonchalantly through the centuries down that peaceful little bit. I knew quite well that if we carried our canoe around it, we should be the first to do so since time began, and I could not endure the silent mockery of all our forerunners.

"Why, of course we'll run it," I said. "There's nothing to it."

Tom looked around again for one second.

"All right, you're the boss," he said. "But if we get through here alive, I want you to land me. Then you can take your old boat plump to hell with you." He faced ahead again.

He was in deadly earnest. I was very much irritated myself. Calling the canoe a *boat*! For half a cent I would turn back and call the whole thing off.

Down the worst of it we went without any mishap. Over the smooth green V that marked the drop, in through the narrow gap in the shelf, with four or five inches to spare. Then the keel caught on a submerged rock and we teetered crazily. There was enough of the canoe ahead of the point at which we had caught to keep the direction true; hence, we were in no immediate danger of damage. We sat for a moment, doing nothing.

Just here the water on each side would be perhaps five feet deep; no depth at all in a quiet stream, but a very different matter with the current as swift as this was. Apparently we were resting on a miniature peak, for there was no projection of the rock on either side of the canoe. There was nothing upon which to stand to lighten the load and so float the craft.

"What do you want me to do?" Tom yelled.

"Nothing! Just keep your shirt on!" I yelled back.

It was not brilliant repartee, but consider the circumstances. They called for wisdom, not wit, and these are seldom found together, wit and wisdom.

Certainly there was nothing Tom could do but sit still. He was doing that, but if ever a man's motionless back, including the back of his head, expressed downright blazing fury, his did. As for me, I could only crawl forward, and hope that the shifting of the weight might release the canoe. I gingerly brought in my paddle, grasped the gunwales with either hand, and began to ease myself ahead until I was stretched out full length over our piles of supplies, face downward. Just after I passed over the tent bundle and was beginning to crush the bread bag, the canoe freed itself and swept on down the stream, the most unguided craft that ever navigated swift water, for the steersman was sprawled out helplessly in an attitude of complete prostration.

We slowed down and I began to right myself. Tom looked round. He had known nothing of all my change of position, and for an instant he appeared startled. Then he turned to watch the canoe and fended it away from the bank towards which it was drifting. I regained my place and dipped my paddle into the quiet water. Tom turned again, a broad grin overspreading his face. Then he began to laugh. We both laughed, loud and long.

"Say, if you'll promise to lie on your belly every time we run a rapids, I guess I'll stay with the expedition," said Tom. "It's only when you try to steer that we get on the rocks."

I do not remember how far our next run of straight paddling extended. My log calls it a "short paddle," and I recall that the warning hum, like the sound of wind rising among the trees, came annoyingly soon, and increased with disconcerting rapidity. Again Tom looked back anxiously. I shook my head. Already I could see the water ahead tumbling white where the river narrowed sharply and made an abrupt turn into the bush. The railroad was again in sight. I scanned both shores of the river. We were near the right bank, but just here the stream widened to a broad pond before it plunged into the heavily-wooded gorge. Then I saw, away across the pond, and much too near the rapids, the welcome fire placard that marks the beginning of a portage. I called to Tom to confirm my surmise, with his younger and better vision. Yes, there was a yellow sign. Tom was all for fetching a very long compass round, lest we should be swept down the rapids in getting over to the other side. When we had crossed, and were resting alongside the log from which we were to unload the canoe, we looked at the wild turmoil of water roaring below us, and turned with relief to the drudgery of a half-mile double carry along the railroad. When we put into the water once more, the river was loitering on its way in complete forgetfulness of its recent agitation.

The next rapids were far away. We paddled steadily on—five, ten, twenty minutes, until I almost entertained the fantastic notion, belied by all my previous experience on the same river, that we were beyond the last of the Petawawa troubles. Finally the river grew wider and there appeared to be a bay or second channel, we could not tell which. Across its mouth lay an orderly line of logs. We were evidently on the heels of a timber drive, and indeed the next turn revealed the rear of the drive itself, with a boom now across the whole river. We cruised beside this, and after several vain attempts to squeeze between the chained ends of the boom logs, we found at last a link in which the chain was low enough in the water, and the log itself sufficiently depressed, to allow us to ease the canoe over by a series of clumsy, spasmodic jerks like the attempts of an undecided young duck to take off from a lake surface. Worming our way among the logs was slow work, especially since we were compelled to paddle across the current in order to reach the fire sign that marked our next carry. Tom was inclined to believe that the logs were intelligently malevolent and eager to stave us in. Below us, where the white water gleamed once more, we could see the drivers busy by the shore. A four-minute portage over a broad, easy trail, with a carpet of pine needles and a blood-thirsty myriad of mosquitoes, thrilled us with our first bush carry.

An eight-minute paddle, a five-minute carry through the bush, and we came out upon a peaceful lagoon. We were close to the railroad again, and straight ahead, across the lagoon, was a dainty wooded point. I shouted. I knew the spot. The year before, Jim and I had made an arrangement with a piratical section gang to transport us as far as possible on the handcar. The point ahead was the place from which we had set out with the canoe. We should soon be turning up into God's own unspoiled country. Quietly we swung over to the right until we found the Creek mouth. A miniature estuary it was, level and peaceful, slipping modestly into the Petawawa, timidly, like a small child silently putting its hand into an adult's.

Less than five minutes of this, and again we heard the familiar roar of water too much hurried in its career. Here was the lowest in a series of old dams, and for us it provides a pleasantly definite beginning for the Creek. All beginnings and ends are but arbitrary terms of convenience, and if we choose to begin a beloved creek with a definite dam, instead of with a more or less uncertain widening, no one may say us nay. I understand from the maps that the authorities wish to have it take its rise far away in a fished-out, four-flusher lake which is not even on the main route. Let 'em. For us, the Creek begins where we enter it.

Here we had our first "lift." A lift is an annoyance. It has no dignity, no character. It is nondescript. By definition, which is the recognized method of concealing inner truth by means of superficial accuracy, a lift is a carry too short to justify all the preparations for a portage proper. The canoe is not carried on the shoulders of one man, but right-side up, in the hands of two, with the lighter parcels left in it. Hence the name. A lift may be fifty yards, or more, or less, in length. It is a minor misery. In the first place, a canoe, carried over uneven ground or rock by two men at different levels and with different methods of handling their respective ends of the craft, and bumping against its carriers, is not only an exceedingly awkward object, but it takes on also an apparent increase in weight that gives each of its bearers an unreasoning but immediate and ineradicable sense of being exploited. Bags and packs are never properly arranged, but are dragged across in a haphazard fashion which doubles the labour and trebles the irritation. Rods are not taken down, nor little odds and ends packed into the big bundles. All in all, a lift is a messy affair. It takes time, and returns very little distance for this time, for often enough the water at the other end is easily visible, just a few ridiculous yards ahead.

Now that I bethink me, this is not the place for a tirade against lifts, for with us, on this occasion, the carry became a lift through an evil chance. We tried to make it a portage. I do not remember whether I had forgotten the shortness of the carrying distance, or whether I thought it easier to carry the canoe alone. I do remember that I lashed the paddles, shouted exultantly to Tom that we were on our way at last, hoisted the canoe to my shoulders, and started briskly up the steep, smooth ridge of rock. Alas! like one Heedless, that was a-going that way, I watched not well my steps. Up the rock, and over the crest, and before me lay a twelve-inch drop which I must have judged to be half that, if I judged at all. I came down with a thud and a grunt, but without falling. It did not matter; indeed, I think I might better have fallen. I have already mentioned that the distance between the thwarts used in carrying was more than ordinarily long. This put a very heavy stress on the paddles at any time of portage. The additional strain of a sudden jolt was too much for paddles already somewhat old, and still suffering from the effects of a long year's drying-out in a furnace-heated cellar. There was a sharp crack, not very loud. There must, in fact, have been two, but the synchronization was perfect. I called to Tom, who helped me lower the canoe gingerly, not to say tenderly, to the ground. Then we unlashed the paddles.

They had not been broken in any coarse, uncompromising manner, but each had been daintily shivered, cracked in a way that made one of them quite useless as a beast of burden or a practical propellent, and the other too delicate to be trusted fifty yards from shore in the most placid of waters. Tom looked at me gravely but said nothing. It must have been nearly one o'clock, and we had not eaten since half-past six. Moreover, not fifteen minutes before, we had felicitated each other quite formally on the approach of lunch. But now, in the face of our calamity, we had no thought of food. By this, of course, I mean that I had no thought of food. Not until this moment of writing, of emotion recollected in comparative tranquillity, did it ever occur to me to wonder if perhaps Tom retained his sensation of hunger.

I thought several futile thoughts. I remembered the advice to take a spare paddle—and cursed the advisers. They had merely embittered the moment. I resolved that I would always be considerate, and never offer advice, to embitter the moments of others. I thought of Robinson Crusoe—cross my heart! I did—and his patient whittling away at two sides of a huge tree until he had whittled it down to a plank. With a grisly fascination in the picture, I saw Tom and me patiently whittling down trees, huge trees, to make paddles, in order to paddle back to that railway bridge, a mile from Radiant. I remembered an account

I had read of men paddling five hundred and sixty miles with their hands, and wondered if we should begin at once to paddle back down the Creek and across the Petawawa, to flag a train. Since the railroad was not more than half a mile away, this would not have involved any great exertion or hardship, but to my morbid thinking it seemed an indefinite, cruelly prolongable ordeal. I suppose that all this was self-laceration, to avoid the clear facing of my folly in being unprepared for such an accident.

I doubt sometimes if Tom has as vivid an imagination as I have, if he is as fully a creative artist. Certainly his behaviour at this time did not proclaim the free creative spirit that moves among the wrecks of time and space, harrowed by the jangle of discordant spheres, and finally, with a wild cry of sorrow for a disordered world, mingled with an exultant shout of artistic parturition, arises and moulds the universe anew, nearer to the heart's desire. The great creative artist flings the broken world aside and builds again. If he cannot create afresh, he knows there is nothing left to do save weep and howl aesthetically. That's me. But it is not Tom. Poor fellow! He knows no better than to mend the broken world and set it going once again.

"S'pose there's any pine around here?" he asked. He had been examining the less damaged of the two paddles.

"Why?"

"You know, if I had some pitch and some thread, or string, or something, I believe I could wrap this one up so it would work, and maybe the other one."

Tom was so romantic, wanting pine pitch, like an ancient Huron or a pioneer in the Queen's bush. He's always half-pretending he's a brave. I fished out our canoe-mending stuff, a tarry substance, which he pronounced ideal. It should have been at the top of my little haversack, but was not. I found also a half-rotted line, which might have been kept until some day the mythical monster trout would break it under maddening circumstances. On a short carry, at least one rusty tin can always lies near the trail. I discovered it and its cover. We built a little fire, arranged the material, and set to work. The difficult factor in handling the canoe-mender is that it must be boiling hot to run, and will not remain boiling hot for more than four seconds in the open air, which is the only kind usually available in such cases. I kept it boiling in the rusty cover, and transferred it, under instructions, to the shivered paddle. We poured it into the splits. Then Tom wound the decrepit line around the paddle, and I poured the boiling mender on it, and smoothed that boiling mender with my fingers. It remained painfully hot long after the four seconds of its running time. Tom's wrapping was so beautiful that I was reluctant to smear the tarry mess over it, but in the course of a marvellous repair job the paddle grew firm once more, until finally Tom pronounced it good. It was good. It is now only a spare, but it carried us up and down rapids all that trip, and over stormy lakes, and it is still as seaworthy as need be. Not only so, but that tinkering wizard wound the other paddle into serviceable submission. He lifted it up at last and shook it. He pressed the blade against the ground. Then he handed it to me.

"I'm starved!" cried Tom. "Let's eat."

But first we carried all our stuff over the ridge, and laid it down near the far end of the lift. Then we boiled our billy of tea, and fried our bacon, and Tom dropped back to cook's assistant, and rummaged for the butter and the bread, and with the egg-beater mixed some Klim in the smallest billy, and put on the dish-water.

> "*Look down, look down that lonesome road,*
> *Befo' you travel on,*"

he sang.

So we were very merry, and leaned back on our elbows on the warm rock, and looked out over that barren, burnt piece of country in the healing heat of the June afternoon sun, and blessed the Lord. With this meal our emancipation had begun. Beyond the ridge, a bare hundred yards away, were people, and cities, and routine, and care, and clamour, and the smell of gasoline, and foul coal-smoke, and houses, but we were now utterly separate from them. We should be eating meals much more remote from civilization than this one, but not again were we to be so conscious of release as in that happy hour. Custom would stale even this bright bliss.

ON THE TRAIL, PARDNER

CHAPTER III

THERE WAS nothing to compel us to go on. I know men who count that day lost in which they have not paddled far into the night, who are happy only when making camp on an unknown spot long after dark and preferably in the rain, who become embittered over their inability to continue doing each day five miles more than they did on the previous day. We are not of their number. If possible we plan our day with a very generous eye to comfort. We hope to make camp an hour and a half or so before sunset, thus leaving time to set up the tent, cook our meal, and wash the dishes—all before the dusk fishing begins.

Now it is true that the afternoon was still young, and there were easily two hours to go. Already, however, we had been on the trail long enough to satisfy an unambitious, city-softened pair of non-athletic men. There was a fair camp-site, uninspiring, unromantic, and too much fire-smitten to be very sylvan, but habitable, with a promise of fish in the waters below the dam.

We did not even discuss the possibility of camping. Some few miles up the Creek were the Forks, and although, as I hinted earlier in this narrative, we had pretended, for fear of disappointment, and to benumb the apprehensions of the long trail, that we did not intend to make the Forks that night, there had been a message between us, unconscious, unacknowledged, but unmistakable, somewhere after that first mile along the railroad, a television message which showed the two of us, fishing in the evening of that day below the dark, scabby apron of the old chute at the Forks.

"Well, had we better be on the way?" I asked.

Tom nodded and began to pack the dishes in the clean-dishes sack. In ten minutes we were paddling steadily but placidly up a lazy creek that meandered between flat, sedgy banks so slowly that it scarcely made the paddling stiffer. For a time, in that warm rich afternoon contentment, we ate the lotus, and purpose became blunted, and there seemed no urge to fish in twilight waters. But even as the spell was being laid, Tom broke it.

"Push over right!" he shouted. "There's a rock. No, I mean left."

In ordinary civilian life, Tom can discern his right hand from his left, but in a canoe upon a stream he is utterly unreliable in this matter. I was slow in making the discovery, and the poor old canoe lost many a patch of paint before I learned my lesson. I have learned it now: I know that when he yells "Rock on right!" there is almost an even chance that the rock will prove after all to be on the right. It is probably fifty feet away, however, and except in swift water there will be time for cross-examination.

There was a rock, about a foot below the surface, and Tom's peace had been destroyed. For we had been paddling through long, slender, grass-like stuff that sloped gently downstream and lay along the surface of the water like a field of tall grain bending before a breeze. Tom cherished a superstition, based on a misplaced confidence in nature's sense of propriety, that no wolfish rocks could lurk among those pastoral scenes. He is an extremist, and now insists that the pleasant little grassy bits are most treacherous of all. At any rate, the dreaming was over, and with it the enjoyment of this peace was gone. We were actually relieved when we heard again that sound which we were coming to distinguish more and more quickly from the sound of the wind in the trees, that murmur that set us watching for portage signs.

It was merely another lift, a proper one this time, but it gave Tom his first major excitement not connected with rapids. He had gone over ahead of me.

"Hey!" he called back. "Isn't this beaver work?"

"I'll be along in a minute," I replied.

It was beaver work. There was no sign of a dam, and not much cutting, but the evidence of recent activity was plain. Several small stumps; two or three fallen trees, with limbs cut off; scattered chips. Tom picked up a handful of chips, but immediately threw them down again. Close to the water lay a section of poplar, about three feet long and between four and five inches in diameter. Why the beavers had cut it out of the felled tree to which it belonged and then left it, I could not guess. Tom could. It had been left as a souvenir for him to carry out with him.

"But that's a log," I protested. "You can't tote that thing all over the bush with you."

"Who says I can't?" Tom replied. "Sure it's a log. It's my beaver log. I like a souvenir that can't be swept up into a dishpan any minute, or dusted off a table."

He put his beaver log ahead of his seat in the bow, so that he could admire it. We paddled, more heavily now, for half an hour or more, until again the warning murmur came to us.

"The long portage," I announced with finality.

Tom looked over to the west.

"We've got nice time to do it in," he said, cheerfully.

We landed. The black flies, not very lively at midday, were beginning the bloodthirsty activities which make a man a shambles from five o'clock till dark, during the long, lovely June evenings in the Algonquin woods. The mosquitoes were about the same as usual, that is, hellish. We frantically covered our exposed areas with fly-dope, pulled on the canvas gardening gloves we had bought against this day, adjusted the netting round our hatbands, ready to drop veils of double thickness down over our shoulders, as soon as we should be really on the trail. I proceeded to cut two short poles. Our repaired paddles could not be used to support the weight of the canoe on the portage. I had refused to burden the expedition with spare paddles: now I had the unpleasant prospect of lugging two poles everywhere or cutting fresh ones at the beginning of each portage. This involves more work than might be expected. In an area given over entirely to trees, I used fondly to assume that trees for any purpose of simple camping would be easily procurable. But I have gone two hundred yards in dense growth to find a tent-pole, and I am not fastidious. Poles for carrying the canoe had to be carefully chosen, and however well selected, they were still inferior to paddles. Ah, well! We took special care with the lashing of the poles. Since we should not be coming back for the canoe until morning, we turned it over.

There was a quiet and impressive earnestness about our setting forth. We were becoming a little tired, and we knew that before we should have covered the two and a half miles between us and the Forks we should be utterly weary. Not that the length was excessive. Seven months ago last Wednesday, Tom and I did a three-and-a-half-mile carry, and then went back for the second load in the evening. But that was at the sorrowful end of our holiday for last summer, and we were toughened. Let me be oracular for a moment. Believe no man who tells you that two miles and a half will not distress the tenderfoot. As you value your life, health and the pursuit of happiness, go not into the bush with such an one.

We knew all this. We knew we were to absent us from felicity awhile. Hence, there was a touch of dignified acceptance of pain about us, dignity being still possible, before the discomfort became too real. I hope we were not too consciously heroic about it, but I admit there used to be something of exaltation in feeling we were undertaking something voluntarily which not every Dick and Harry (I must omit Tom) would care to do.

"We'll do twenty minutes and rest five," I proclaimed.

"Okay," said Tom, and began to load up.

I wriggled my arms into the straps of my pack, shook it straight, and staggered to my feet.

"Ready?"

"Okay," said Tom.

"Well, we're off."

The restraints imposed by modesty on first person narrative prevent me from doing justice to the dramatic expressiveness of that last remark. Those who have done long portages, especially young amateurs, will understand.

The most disturbing aspect of any distress is the element of uncertainty as to duration. Nowhere is this truer than on a bush trail. I have devised various ameliorations. Perhaps others in the woods employ similar devices. I do not know, for I have always felt ashamed of mine, and have never admitted them until now, even to Tom. My favourite is a mathematical self-hypnosis and self-deception, which has served for opiate on many a barely supportable last lap. It is a childish trick, dating from early boyhood. I count. On the trail, in these later years, if I have a load, I do about one hundred steps to the minute, including stumblings and dodgings as steps with the rest. I am thus provided with a method of telling time, a method having very definite value, on account of its inaccuracies.

One of these benign inaccuracies arises because I do slightly fewer than a hundred to the minute. Let us suppose that I wish to know when ten minutes have gone by. It may be I am carrying the canoe, and am to be relieved in ten minutes. I begin counting, and I assume I must count up to a thousand, that is, take one thousand paces, before I shall be relieved. Of course, I never reach the thousand, and to this day I am able to be joyful over the surprise of relinquishing the load too soon. Silly, isn't it? Still, it has the justification of achieving a useful result. But in addition to this constant alleviation, this never-failing hastening of the moment of release, there is a further possibility, a varying unknown factor. Besides counting, one is fighting black flies and mosquitoes, twisting ankles on roots, easing straps off a galled neck, answering occasional remarks, looking at tree trunks, flowers, shrubs, perhaps even thinking about life or something, or recalling a snatch of rhyme. The result is that since each hundred is an independent unit, there comes a time, anywhere from three hundred to seven, when I am quite uncertain as to whether I am ending my four hundreds or just beginning them. The very salutary philosophy of my youth hammered my expectations upon the anvil of experience into a conviction that if at any time I visited the oracle, I ought to take the more sinister interpretation. If I wondered whether or not I had carried in the fire-wood for the night, I had not. If I had doubts as to whether I had gone three or four hundred, I had gone three hundred. As an agreeable consequence, I have more than once been startled to find that I must have done about twice the number of steps my tally indicated. It is amazing, the renewal of cheer and strength such a discovery gives the lonely man on the trail.

For rarely is a man so alone as on the trail, especially under a canoe. He is then shut off completely from his fellow. Tom and I have sat for hours by a camp-fire at night, without a word to each other, each of us thinking his own thoughts, but with a most acute sense of companionship. Meditation is not lonely, even when it is solitary. But on the trail, with a heavy load, and weary, a man is intensely alone. The exertion, the pounding activity, the noise of one's own heavy breathing, of one's own heart beating, the implacable insistence of sweat—all these give something of the loneliness of severe pain, and forbid the soothing attunement of the spirit to the universe, which makes communion out of contemplation. In a sometimes dreadful sense, a man is lonely with his burden on the trail, once it has become a burden, once the buoyancy is gone.

I began to count. At two thousand there would be a rest, unless Tom suggested it before then. There was no call to start off too briskly; we should only tire the sooner. It was a pleasant trail, but it bothered me vaguely. Thirty-three, thirty-four. Could we get to the Forks in time for fishing? Fifty-seven, fifty-eight. Pine needles are beautiful, but if they are too thick and dry, they supply poor traction on a slope. Eighty-five, eighty-six. Ouch! How had that mosquito got at my back there? My shirt-tail must have slipped up again and left a gap above my corduroys. Two hundred and sixty. Would he bring the car to Opeongo to meet us all right? Would he forget to put water in the radiator? Ninety-eight, ninety-nine, a hundred; that is three hundred. Or was it two hundred? No, it was more than two hundred. Six, seven, eight. Four hundred. Five hundred. And twenty. It was going to be a hard trip, but anyway there was half a thousand of it done. How many would there be altogether?

Thirty-five, forty. Then a sickening shock, and a mocking memory. The trail was leading directly down to the Creek again. We were not yet on the long trail at all. I should have remembered this short carry: I remembered it quite well now. There was no need to tell Tom, for he had seen it almost as soon as I had. Life, however, has dealt him some shrewd knocks, and disappointed expectations do not really surprise him. He looked again towards the west, from the open place by the Creek, as soon as he laid his packs down. Our fishing hour at the other end was vanishing.

ON THE TRAIL, PARDNER

Silently we plodded back over the trail for the canoe and the second load. I had grown suddenly tired. Tom offered to take the canoe over, but I refused. The tradition was that a man carried his own canoe on a short portage. That was the devil of it. It was a short portage.

Silently, as far as Tom was concerned, and sullenly, as far as I was, we loaded the canoe again and set out. In five minutes we had both renewed our spirits. After all, we were not compelled to reach the Forks. We could camp anywhere when night came. Twenty, perhaps thirty minutes, and the sound that was not a rustling murmured from the deepening growth ahead. Tom looked back at me; I grinned and nodded. There she was at last.

The grin and the cheerfulness faded when we reached the sign. The abrupt, rocky rise, almost immediately from the water, showed even Tom the novice that this was no long carry. It was a trivial lift.

Now I was bewildered. I had been over this same trail exactly a year before, to the very day, and already I had utterly forgotten a portage and a lift. Not only had I forgotten their existence, but I had definitely remembered their non-existence. It was not the extra labour involved; it was the shattering of all assurance, all confidence. How many more of the damned things were there?

Again we put into the Creek. I do not know how long we paddled—not long—before we came into a stiffly resisting current. We laboured on into shoaling waters, on to where a little sandbar divided the stream. Hopeful memory began timidly to reassert itself.

"Are we going to the left here?" Tom shouted.

"No, the right."

We swung out, crept round the end of the island, and pushed ourselves along, beside a fallen birch that almost blocked the upper entrance to the left channel. Past that, a miniature bay of quietness received us, and a grassy shore, and a yellow sign. I needed no sign. I knew the island, the birch, the miniature bay of quietness, the grassy shore.

"That's her, Tom," I said.

"Fine," said Tom. "Will I get out first?"

I was greatly relieved, of course, to know that we had arrived at a recognized spot, but the question of camping was now to be considered. We were tired; the sun was low; the trail led through a thick growth that would darken the path early. The flies and mosquitoes were viciously active, worse by far than at Radiant. About thirty or forty yards from the landing I could see two long sticks, crossed; undoubtedly tent-poles. Here was a camping-place, and someone had used it. There was all day tomorrow for getting to the Forks.

"Tom," I said, "had we better camp here, and go on in the morning?"

"Okay," said Tom. "It looks as if somebody else did, up the trail a piece. But I'm all right to go on if you want to."

Tom always seemed to regard the expedition as mine, with the irritating result that at times it was quite impossible to discover his own inclinations. This was one of the times. He is a man of few words, except in his winter reminiscences, and I knew the futility of discussion. We smeared fly-dope over ourselves. We lit our pipes—at least I lit mine, and Tom rolled a cigarette. We looked at each other.

"Aw heck!" said Tom. "Let's go on."

It was word-perfect telepathy, and it electrified us both. Weariness fell away, with the passing of indecision. Again we distributed our stuff for a long carry and a non-return that night. For instance, we put all the bread but one loaf under the canoe. When we set out this time, it was without any dramatic emotion. There was urgency, too much practical urgency, for the dramatic. Moreover, we were becoming half-conscious of the need for conserving energy of every kind. Nevertheless, Tom took his beaver log. He must have imagined that someone might steal it.

I began to count paces, of course. Indeed, I tried to work out a sort of comparative table of steps and yards. It was not very successful, since I lacked one necessary bit of information, the length of my bush step. I have watched my father and others pace off a distance and announce the result with an air of calm assurance that invariably caused a hasty and furtive putting away of rules and tape-lines. At times I have essayed it myself, but mostly in the presence of females only, and always where the question of distance was purely academic. I think it was an artificial step, a kind of measuring goose-step, which these experts used. I know it was not the step of the tired greenhorn on the ups and downs of a darkening bush trail running over rocks and bits of rotting corduroy, and through oozy, muddy dells, and among roots. I forget how far I had gone in my reduction of steps to miles, yards, feet and inches, when I decided to give up the effort.

The trail is really not bad. As trails go in most regions of the north country, it is almost a highway; and even for the Park, it is good. If ever I feel critical of it, I need only remind myself of the old portage from Dickson Lake to Bondfield. The trail to the Forks follows a disused tote-road, abandoned by the lumbermen some fifty years ago or more, but still very superior as to width and undeviousness. The worst places are not far from the lower end, the end from which we were now starting. The road had originally skirted the bank of the Creek, and in two places a bit of timbered work eked out a scanty width. The wood in this has rotted, and it is now in a state of treacherous decay and equally treacherous declivity. We stumbled, to be sure, but as both the ancient works are within the first half-mile, we made light of them and waxed almost jocular.

That was the last flicker of gaiety—and a pallid gaiety it was. Then the burden descended upon us, and we plodded. I do not know what Tom thought about. I have never asked him. As for me, I continued to count, though not to reduce arithmetically. Also I meditated bitterly on the idiocy of men who leave comfort and domestic amenities for this unspeakable slavery. I thought of the reluctance with which I would walk, carrying nothing, to the corner drug-store at home, eight minutes away. The only occasions on which I could recall walking to that corner were when the car was out of kilter. I remembered my age, and the wise old saw that tells us there is no fool like an old fool.

I would step down suddenly, and jolt loose every tooth in my head, including those that had grown there. The black flies burrowed inside my shirt. As I would reach behind my ears to dislodge some of them from that favourite lunch-counter, my hand would come back half-covered with blood. I plastered myself again with fly-dope, and had a respite of a few minutes, until my violent sweating washed away the greater part of the repellent. I began to limp. I knew I had a blister, and I swore that never again would I try to finish wearing out a pair of city shoes in the bush. I swore that I would never wear any shoes, or anything else, in the bush again, so help me. I may say that I did remember the first part of that lesson, to the slight

ON THE TRAIL, PARDNER

benefit of those destitute who apply to the Salvation Army for assistance.

A snatch of a silly old song, forgotten, as I thought, a quarter-century before, came leering back to plague me.

> *Good morning, Mr. Mulligan,*
> *I hear the neighbours shout.*
> *La la la la la la la la*
> *La la la la la la lout,*
> *The birds they were a-singing*
> *When I wheeled the baby out.*

I did not utter a sound, but that infernal fragment kept revolving in my mind. I tried frantically to remember other songs, to exorcize the demon.

> *On a tree by a willow*
> *A little tomtit*
> *Sang willow, tit willow, tit willow.*
> *La la la la la la la*
> *La la la la la la lout,*
> *The birds they were a-singing*
> *When I wheeled the baby out.*

> *Come young, come old, come all draw nigh,*
> *Come listen to my story.*
> *I'll tell you of a plan I found*
> *To catch young Katie Morey.*
> *Ri toe i ree, ri toe ree,*
> *Ri toe i ree ri toe.*
> *La la la la la la la*
> *When I wheeled the baby out.*

> *Fear no more the heat o' the sun,*
> *Nor the furious winter's rages;*
> *Thou thy worldly task hast done,*
> *Home art gone and ta'en thy wages.*
> *Golden lads and girls all must,*
> *As chimney-sweepers, come to dust.*

But with that the dreadful wheel ceased turning, stopped by a more compelling spell than the diabolical witchcraft I had been enduring. Not because of any special familiarity with *Othello*, but because an exquisite little bit from a speech of Iago was used as a filler in one of my school readers, it now came to my mind, after the song from *Cymbeline*.

> *Good name in man or woman, dear my lord,*
> *Is the immediate jewel of their souls:*
> *Who steals my purse, steals trash; 'tis something, nothing;*
> *'Twas mine, 'tis his, and has been slave to thousands;*
> *But he that filches from me my good name*
> *Robs me of that which not enriches him,*
> *And makes me poor indeed.*

I am convinced that rarely has a great thought been more inept than at the moment when that one came to me, for never was a good name a more utterly useless possession than at that hour on the trail to the Forks. It was not more worthless than my purse, which had no value whatever in the bush, but it was equally trashy.

Not that this mattered. My desperate mind clung to those words, and I reiterated them a hundred times, in conjunction with my counting, which continued incessantly. I assure you that it does not require an active brain to do what I am describing.

At the end of the chapter in *Ivanhoe* which tells of the death of the redoubtable though unpleasant Front-de-Bœuf there is naturally a concluding sentence. It runs thus: "But it were impious to trace any farther the picture of the blasphemer and parricide's deathbed." You will recall that the author left off at a point which a modern writer would regard as the end of the general introduction. At one stage in my development, I cursed Sir Walter Scott for those words of ancient decency; later, I became reconciled; now, I bless him. I am not suggesting a parallel between the two situations, but I do point out that I have respectable if antiquated precedent for skipping the chronicle of my further delirium.

Finally, of course, I realized that I had been on this trail since time began, and that I should still be on it when eternity became bored with itself. I realized that time was standing still, that in some mysterious way space had caught up with me, and that, like poor Alice, I needed all the walking I could do to stay in the same place. I even reached the point at which illusory landmarks, false indications that we were near the end, ceased to enrage me. The sun had long since set, the shadows had merged into each other, night was almost upon us, when we stumbled into an open space where a faint light still lingered. I stopped, as soon as I came out from the sombreness through which we had been moving, and waited for Tom.

"Are we here?" he asked, as he dumped his load and fell in a heap upon it.

I cannot imagine why I needed his direct question to bring me out of my delusion. I told myself that this had to be the place. I knew very well it was not.

I looked at Tom and groaned. He grunted. Then a cool little breeze, given a bit of elbow-room in this clearing, played across my drenched face. With it came the first return of hope. I thought I remembered something.

"Wait here," I said to Tom. "I'll go on just a little piece without the load."

"Why?" he asked. Then he added, "Okay."

I walked on through the clearing, into the trail again, and began to run. I fell, and picked myself up, gasping. Three hundred steps I would go. After fifty I slowed into a walk, sometimes a painful crawl. At just over the count of two hundred I broke through into the open again, and bumped against a crude sort of table, on the left side of the trail. I was at the Forks.

Tom said nothing when I told him. Twice his top bundle fell off; three times he had to build up his load. We could still see dimly along the trail.

We must have found tent-poles somehow, but I have no recollection of our setting up the tent in the grass. I remember crawling inside and fastening the tent-fly amid a pandemonium of mosquitoes. I remember Tom holding the flashlight while I sprayed the tent. I remember the almost instantaneous silence, and the incredible cessation from struggle.

"Let's just eat something cold," I said.

"Okay," said Tom, "but I believe I'd like to just rest a couple of minutes first. I'm not very hungry now. Will I get you the bread?"

"No," I said, "I'll lie down a minute too."

We pulled off our shoes. I partially unrolled my blanket, pushed my big pack into position to rest my head on it, and extended myself in a satisfying stretch of utter relaxation, feebly kicking one shoe out of the way.

"I'll get myself an orange in a minute," I thought, "and Tom an onion and some jam for his bread. It's too dark to find anything without the flashlight."

I am convinced that I heard Tom snore. Tom swears that on the contrary he heard me.

AT THE FORKS

CHAPTER IV

Tom's side of the tent was still dark, but my slope of canvas was white, as white as its mildew streaks and generally unwashed condition allowed it to become.

"So that is where the east is!" I thought. "I am sure that was north last year."

Then I became awake, and remembered that I had not gone to bed properly, and felt shivery and aching and mussy. I glanced idly over towards Tom. An untidy and unhygienic heap is usually all that can be seen, for Tom has a barbarous habit of pulling his bedclothes completely over his head in the early hours of the morning. There would be no untidy heap this morning, but I was startled to see no heap, no Tom at all. I listened: had he started the fire? But I could hear none of the cheery, quiet crackling that betrays even the smallest of newly-kindled morning fires. Then I heard my name whispered. The fly of the tent opened slightly, and Tom looked in.

"Come out quick," he said, and disappeared.

I had only to put on my shoes and mackinaw jacket. A mist hung over the little clearing, not very heavy up here by the tent, but thicker lower down, where Tom was standing still by the water's edge.

At the Forks, the tumultuous little Crow River, known in this account as the Creek, tumbling down its narrow valley from the west, is joined by the sluggish White Partridge, lolling from the south-east through a reedy, lily-ponded marsh. Above the Forks this marsh, a quarter-mile to half a mile in width, extends straight and open to the view for a mile or more before a pine-covered bluff cuts it off. Below the Forks, the reinforced stream plunges wildly through two and a half miles of foaming gorges, in a series of cascades so uninterrupted that nowhere could a small chip come to rest for a breathing moment.

Tom was peering through the mist on the White Partridge marsh. He pointed excitedly towards a number of black stumps looming uncertainly out of the semi-opaqueness, perhaps a hundred yards away. As I watched them, one of the stumps stirred, then another. At that moment the haze lifted slightly, enough to throw the objects into less blurred outline. Tom turned to me, inquiringly.

"Moose," I said.

"There's five of 'em!" he whispered. "I've been watching 'em."

Incredulously, I gazed into the mist, now thickening again. Sure enough, I could see that five of the objects moved, and there was no question of their identity. Tom had never before seen a moose in the bush, but I had frequently been thrilled by them in earlier years north of Sault Ste. Marie. Though I had promised Tom plenty of deer, I had not dared to mention moose. Jim and I in two trips into these same regions had never caught a glimpse of those mysterious, uncouth giants. Five of them! Many a morning, similar to this one, I had been happy to count experience, which I seemed not to do. Never, after that first morning, was my porridge unsalted, rarely was it underdone, and not very often was it too thin. We both like it stiff enough to mould. But I maintain to this day it is purely an accident if Tom mixes the correct quantity of Klim. He invariably gives us too much, and then professes an unconvincing passion for it as a beverage, in order not to throw any of it away. We have thrown it away, but always guiltily. A frugality inherited through a hundred generations of necessitous ancestors deprives us of the joy of exuberant wastefulness at any time. In the bush, of course, there is always the tingling possibility of unforeseen scarcity to fortify with reasons our uncomfortable instinct.

We ate our breakfast; we washed the dishes; we put twelve prunes to soak.

It was still not later than half-past six. In theory, there remained nearly three good fishing hours, but the tackle was unfortunately two and a half miles away, at the lower end of the trail, under our overturned canoe. We lamented this fact, honestly on Tom's part, hypocritically on mine. Up to that time I had never had luck with early morning fishing in these waters anyway; nor, I may add, have I had any since, though I have fished every hour from pre-dawn grey to blazing noon.

During the excitement of watching the herd of moose and of getting the first real breakfast we had been unconscious of stiffness and soreness, but during the tedium of dish-washing we had become acutely aware of all the complaining muscles that had been loafing for fifty weeks. Mine, at any rate, had been loafing for fifty weeks. Accordingly, the prospect of travelling that savage trail, to pick up the canoe and the rest of our stuff, did not appeal to either of us. We invented excuses for delay. The grass was wet with a heavy dew. To be sure, except for a little clearing close to the camp, there was no grass on the trail. We made much of seeking undrenched spots for airing the blankets, which could quite happily have waited until the process of evaporation had taken care of the dew, as it normally did.

At last we started off, about half-past nine, I judge. As I might have remembered, the trail was a joy and a delight, actually one of the most pleasant of all the trails we follow in the Park. It is very wide and free of clambering. It winds along its needle-covered way, accompanying the madly plunging Creek, sometimes at a coy and almost silent distance, sometimes in boisterous proximity. What in the threatening darkness of the night before had given me a sensation of claustrophobia, now seemed the very cosy intimacy of close-arching foliage. It was all refreshing, resinous, resilient; our fatigue fell from us like the burden from the back of Christian. We timed ourselves at the end of the trail. Fifty-five minutes. Easy—nothing to it. Pooh! Pooh!

In this same light-hearted or light-headed spirit we started back. Ten minutes on the canoe, ten minutes on the sundries. We had only one watch. The man carrying the lighter load carried also the watch. At the end of the period he would call out, "Time!" The canoe-carrier would ground the nose of the canoe, pull his head out from between the paddles, and wait, supporting the canoe on his hands. The relief man would come behind the carrier, hold the weight until the other man moved behind him again, and then assume position for taking the canoe. The relieved carrier would help adjust the canoe-pad.

"Got her?"
"Got her."
"Right."

AT THE FORKS

The new carrier would shake the canoe into balance, lurch a step or two, and then swing off down the trail. The old carrier would look at the watch, gather up his stuff, and with a sigh of contentment and a lightened step fall in behind. Usually the new carrier would daub on a fresh application of fly-dope before moving into the comparative defencelessness of his job, since the overturned craft cut off any breeze there might be, imprisoned hordes of whatever insects were current, and at the same time kept a man's hands generally occupied.

Five—seven—eight—nine—ten minutes. The cycle had come round.

"Time's up."

"Right," in a faint and distant voice.

We had a bit of a feud on. Tom had a noble but confusing habit of counting the ten minutes in such a way as to include the time spent in changing, roughly a minute. I preferred to count only actual carrying time. Now it is astonishing how important a minute becomes when one is under a canoe, or rather when one has been under a canoe for several minutes. To be sure, I benefited by this habit of Tom's, but it interfered with my statistics. I had no sure measure of the carrying time from one end of a portage to the other. Besides, decency compelled me to follow his method, since I had no assurance that he was following mine and every suspicion that he was not. It was not entirely decency that compelled me; it was really enlightened self-interest. I learned very early in the canoe-trip game that comfort and joy are dependent upon a consciousness, shared by all, of rigid fairness of distribution.

The ethics of the bush, as I understand them, are not very exalted. Unselfishness is a vice. I have known two unselfish people on camping trips—one selfless, the other aggressively unselfish. They rendered two holidays unhappy, because unfortunately they were not both on the same trip. The selfless one ruined the souls of those members of the party who imposed upon him, and destroyed the comfortable peace of mind of those who did not. The aggressively unselfish one exasperated everybody. Men who go into the bush are earthy and fallible. Their highest ethical value is fair play, which receives as much as it gives, and receives as gladly as it gives cheerfully. They do not succeed in loving their neighbours as themselves, but they do try to treat their neighbours as well as they do themselves, though rarely to the extent of wishing their neighbour to catch quite as fine a trout as they themselves have caught. Should they reach this incredible state, they must be taken out to civilization as soon as possible. They are needed there. Men camping in the bush tend to follow, whether they recognize it or not, a practical imperative which teaches them the dependence of their satisfaction upon the satisfaction of the other man. It may indeed be that their satisfaction is intensified by that of their neighbour, and even by their own attitude of fairness, if they are not too conscious of it in themselves as a moral virtue. The Wheel of being and causation still turns inexorably. I cannot deny that at times the bushwise but unregenerate will content himself with giving his fellow-camper the illusion, the shadow of fair play, without the substance. He probably in such cases deceives himself as to the degree of the illusion.

It was five minutes to twelve when we reached camp. For the last hour Tom had been discussing lunch whenever we had a chance to exchange remarks; I was hungry myself. I had resolved upon an extra slice of bacon each, had determined to open the cheese parcel, had even half-decided on pancakes. But when, beside the trail in front of the tent, I dropped the canoe and unfastened the carrying-pad, I saw Tom lay down the bundle that contained the fishing tackle. Only fifty yards away were trout; here at last was the tackle.

"Say we take five minutes and just throw in a line. They won't bite at noon, but it won't take five minutes to try it out."

"Fine," said Tom.

We set up the rods. Tom put the landing-nets together; I got out the fly-book. That fly-book bothered me, for it was new. Though only Tom was there to see, I felt as self-conscious as an average man with a new suit of clothes. In fact, there was more than the ordinary sense of shameful conspicuousness connected with new apparel. Throughout the trip I was trading heavily on my rôle of veteran, into which rôle the presence of a distressingly new fly-book seemed to me to inject a very awkward element. I had even thought of smudging it to produce an artificial aging, but dim memories of something I had once read and admired in Ruskin hindered me. That fly-book remains to this day most provokingly clean and undiscoloured.

I put on a Silver Doctor at the end and a Montreal at the first loop.

"What do you want, Tom?" I asked.

"Flies?" cried Tom. "I wouldn't know what to do with a fly if I had one. I don't believe in flies, anyway. Give me a good lively worm and you can have the flies. Where'd I put that worm box?"

You will not have forgotten that we were now at the Forks, the confluence of the White Partridge and the Creek. There are two fishing holes at this spot, and indeed three, but I have never taken more than two or three little trout from the third, for which cause I disregard it here.

THE INCOMPLETE ANGLERS

The White Partridge is, as I mentioned before, a lazy, marshy stream at this lower end. For the final hundred yards of its independent existence, however, it narrows and grows swift. At the upper end of its narrow part, in the ancient lumbering days, a short sluice was built, through which the logs were led. It has been broken down these forty, fifty years, the water level has fallen, until there is now at the upper end only a confused jumble of rotting timbers and piled-up drift. The water runs, not over, but under the old sluice floor. At the lower end is the first hole, a pool deep enough to be dark, roughly circular in shape, forty yards or so across, its limit below marked by a large rock standing out on the left as you look down. On one flank of this rock is the White Partridge, on the other the Creek.

Standing on the floor, we began to fish. Of course I knew that we could not get fish there at that hour, out in broad sunshine. Of course I was disappointed when nothing rose to my cast. I might as well call it a cast, for lack of a term of accurate definition. If anglers will understand that in using the word I am not claiming the performance, perhaps I may be allowed to use it. Strictly speaking, it was, and is, a process consisting of a fling and a drag. I hurl the fly in the general direction of a trout's possible whereabouts, and then reel in so as to drag the fly along the surface of the water until the last hope fades. Then I repeat the performance. Occasionally I grow ambitious, and try to fling my fly thirty-five or even forty feet. On such occasions, if we are fishing along the Creek, I invariably hook the neighbouring foliage.

Tom was not casting. He was following the usage of his ancestors. He had put on a worm—half a worm, to be exact—and a sinker heavy enough to anchor a scow, and had dropped his load into the brown depths at the very end of the sluice. It always gives me a twinge of jealous fear to see anyone drop a line into that particular spot. We have never taken anything but small trout from that hole, but I have a superstition that one big fellow must lurk just under the sluice. Tom jiggled his line, lifted it and threw it out some twelve or fifteen feet. Then he lit his pipe and sat down on a side wall, but with his line still in the water.

"Tom, do you mind if I slip up to the other hole and just throw the line in once?" I asked.

"No, go ahead," said Tom.

"Come on up with me."

"No, I'll just sit here and smoke and dangle my worm," he replied.

"Yes, forsooth, I wish you joy o' the worm," I said. Tom disdained retort.

It is only seventy or eighty yards from the sluice to the second hole, but the trail is through shrubbery and under spruces with low branches, whereby lines, hooks, landing nets, and other tanglous items become profanely involved. Finally, however, I crawled out from the thicket to the water's edge. This was on the far side of the big rock; hence, the waters were those of the Creek, not of the White Partridge. The Creek comes chasing down in characteristic fashion. It turns just here, and runs for forty or fifty feet parallel with the other stream. On a pebbled bar between them is piled a long heap of whitened driftwood. On the other side of the driftwood the White Partridge flows dark and sullen, though fast. On this side the Creek sparkles down among the stones, clear and gay and reckless with from six to fifteen to twenty inches of water, dances coquettishly up to the very arms of the gaunt old drift, and then purls along beside it to the end of the sandbar, where it must give up its individual career.

The fishing hole is at the elbow. By means of a fair-sized log and a series of more or less reliable stones, some of which, despairing of gathering moss in such an environment, show tendencies to roll, it is possible to get well out into the stream.

I should explain that we had no waders. I have a suspicion that they are expensive; I have never priced them. Since Tom and I are convinced that we cannot afford them, we have added them to the sissified paraphernalia that we despise. Consequently, each year we pass through an almost daily progression while we are on the Creek. If possible, we begin the day with dry feet, that is, with dry socks. We guard the dryness of our feet with a pitiful anxiety, and make vast circuits to avoid wetting them. We step, like Agag, delicately, and test out stones before we commit ourselves to them. Then sooner or later there comes the inevitable minute which awaits us each day: we go in kersplash. There is a moment of profane exasperation; then a huge relief; then a joyous splashing and shouting in the abandon of our new-found liberty. Next day we go out again; dry, circumspect, anxious.

Poised precariously on the largest and outermost stone, I cast out my line. Ping! A flash of silver—a sudden jerk— a fierce clicking of the reel. I had him on! Madly I began to swing the rod from side to side, and to pull it back over my head, in order to keep up with the lengthening line. He must not get under a log. He must not dart under a stone. I must keep the line taut, but not too tight. I must remember not to jerk. I must remember all the painful lessons of former years. Above all, I must try not to reel him in too fast or too short. Finally, I grew collected enough to acquire control of the trout and myself. For the life of me I cannot tell when I actually began to reel in line. I do know that I had put the reel on wrong, and began by giving the trout the advantage of several yards of loose line. He was still on when I caught up again. By this time Tom was watching me, and my joy was full. I had seen my prize. Though it was no monster, it was a good-sized fish. It was putting up the fight that trout in fast water can always give, but it was evidently well hooked. I was impatient to have it landed, however, and began to shorten line. On the right side of the stone on which I was standing, the water was shallower and a bit quieter. Thither I would lead my prey.

There is at this point a difficulty, perhaps confined to me of all fishermen, but not the less real on that account. It is concerned with the co-operation between a rod and a landing-net, or rather with the space-lag between them. To explain this, I must be allowed and forgiven a bit of autobiography. As a boy, I was troubled by no difficulty in this matter. My fishing was all done from the shores of creeks, and was in the main restricted to the twenty-fourth of May. I used to go fishing on that day, not with any real hope of catching fish, but solely because I was permitted to do so, and considered myself bound to exercise any privilege granted me. When I did catch a fish—generally a catfish—I invariably hauled in my line as fast as possible, yanked the fish out of the water with a mighty swing far over the land, and then, if it had not fallen off the hook while still in or over the water, I ran it down as it floundered back towards the stream. This procedure did not provide a use for a landing-net, even if I had owned one. I did not even wish for a landing-net. I had a vague desire for a mysterious implement called a gaff, not from any sense of need, but because an early school reader had mentioned a gaff as somehow connected with fishing.

Throughout my life I have had the embarrassing experience of learning every new skill about nine years after my contemporaries have known it. One result has been an increasing reluctance to admit ignorance of what everybody else has known for years. There is at least one compensation for this. Long after all my fellows have put away childish things, I can still go about with the fresh delight of wonder. Now there never was a time when I did not want to go on canoe trips and to fish. But the first opportunity did not come until I had reached the age when most men are telling their adolescent sons of the heavy portages they could or should or would have taken, or did take, some ten or fifteen years ago. Consequently, I was forced to assume a virtue though I had it not, and rather to allow the conviction of my extreme stupidity and awkwardness to deepen in men's minds, expressed or unexpressed, than to admit that I barely knew which end of the paddle to stick into the water. I doubt now if I have succeeded in deceiving many, but I have never been sent back home. A man cannot be discarded in the middle of a long canoe trip, especially if he is the only other member of the party. Eventually, as was bound to be the case, even I acquired experience of a rough and ready kind.

Accordingly, I had never confessed to anyone that I knew nothing of how to land a fish with a net. Now when the net is in the water and the fish is being led to it, or when the fish is in the water and the net is being guided to it, as the case may be, there ought to be, I think, a nice adjustment of distance, so that these two could be brought neatly and featly together. But I do not achieve this nice adjustment. I find myself reaching out wildly with one hand as far as I can, while with the other I manage to manipulate the rod in such a way as to leave a gap 'twixt fish and net. In my frantic efforts to bridge this gap, I lunge with the net, and I jerk on the rod at the same time with a hand which is usually far out of effective control behind my shoulder. The fish comes hurtling by, some eight or ten inches beyond, or short of, or away from the net. After a time, however, if the fish remains hooked, it is bound to pass over the net. Then I almost invariably pull convulsively on both net and rod, leaving the same gap, but this time in the air above the net. Frequently, I land the fish.

It was during one of these attempts to net this first trout of the expedition that I suddenly felt the strain eased. I swung my rod out of the water: my trout was gone! There comes a time when the loss of a fish is a small matter even to the humble, unless it is demonstrably the best of the season. But that time is never when the first fish is hooked. The sense of desolation, of futility, of the vanity of all vanities, of the utter unlikelihood of catching another one during the whole trip, is quite trying. I realized that I should never have come at all, that I should have stayed home and tried to learn to like to garden, that I had made a failure of my whole life. After a few moments given over to this despair, I reeled my line in, shifted position slightly on my boulder, and prepared to cast again. Tom was not looking at me; he was apparently relighting his pipe. A very decent chap, that Tom.

I threw the line in, naturally at the same spot as before. I let it drift down alongside the logs. I drew it back up the centre of the current; then I cast it on the far side of the current, just at the line that marked the edge of the quieter water. Again the jerk, the click, the tightening. The incredible had happened; I had another. This time a tremendous intensity of purpose slowed my excitement. I was determined to play this trout until it would seek the shelter of the net from sheer exhaustion and a desire to have done with it all. I played it. I guided it back and forth with a dogged persistency that should have been admired. I waited. I could see Tom watching me, and I waved a calm encouragement. Finally I decided that the time had come to net this trout, especially since an uneasy suspicion had begun to trouble me. I preserved my majestic calm, led the line around to the more peaceful side of my rock, and scooped my net accurately. There was no difficulty whatever until I actually had my trout in the net. Then I felt in my pocket for my tape-line. A speckled trout must be at least seven inches long, and this pathetic little infant looked about five.

An honest, law-abiding man, situated so that a game warden is unlikely to appear immediately, beginning a fishing trip of uncertain success, with one fish lost to his disgrace and nothing to his creel—I have no creel, but I like the word—with a passion for trout, and with one six and three-quarter inch fish in his net, is in a serious predicament. My trout was unquestionably seven and a quarter inches long, however, as measurements proved. I took it ashore and laid it reverently down, not without qualms. It did seem very tiny, and it was very beautiful.

As I cast again, after having observed that the Silver Doctor had taken first blood, I had none of the triumphant glow I had expected to accompany my first catch. But almost at once all concern over my sensations and qualms was lost in the excitement of another strike. As I began to play it, and first caught sight of its flashing splendour, all previous time ceased to exist. A tumult pounded and whirled in my head. But when, almost at the same time, another flash broke the water, and I realized that I had two fish hooked, exultation gave place to something very like terror. How could I possibly land two trout, both good ones? How could I possibly land one of the two? I wish I knew how I did land them. I remember the despairing discovery that the bigger one was not on the end hook. After that, I have a confused medley of impressions which become coherent only with the sound of Tom's voice close beside me.

"Did you get 'em both?" he was shouting, as he made his way along the log.

For answer I held up the net. They were undoubtedly and decisively in it.

For some reason, Tom declined my suggestion that he try his luck here. He was not yet ready to accept a fly, and a worm did not seem very likely bait for this kind of water. That was his story, at any rate. He went back to his place on the apron of the sluice, while I resumed my attempts at casting as soon as I had extricated my hooks and line from the meshes of the landing-net. Nothing happened for a time; then, just as I was about to quit, another rose and was hooked. But the tumult and the shouting were over for that day. After the sensational capture of my two, single takes seemed tame. After my seventh there was no more response. I cast a dozen times hopefully; then half a a dozen idly. Finally, I fell back on the only sure device I have for forcing myself away from a fishing hole, the setting of a limit of three casts. I made the casts; I allowed the stream to carry the line as far down as I dared; I dragged the line back as slowly as I could; eventually, I had to reel it in.

Tom had caught nothing, but he concealed his disappointment perfectly. I could only surmise his feelings from what mine would have been under the same circumstances, and I think I did him an injustice.

We looked at the time. It was half-past one.

"It was five minutes we were to fish, wasn't it?" Tom commented.

I have sense enough to refrain from trying to describe the eating of those trout. When I say, modestly and truthfully, that I am the best non-professional camp-fire fish-cook I know; and when I remind the reader that we had had no brook trout for a year, and that the first of these had been caught less than two hours before it went into the pan, I have done all that is necessary for the initiate. The uninitiate could not understand in any case.

Because four of the seven were between twelve and thirteen inches long, I proposed that we cook only four and leave the rest for the next meal. Tom laughed me to scorn.

"Say, I could eat the whole seven myself with one hand tied behind my back," he assured me.

"First thing you know you'll be sick of the sight of trout," I warned him.

AT THE FORKS

"Me sick of trout?—That's not much of a joke, but it's pretty fair for you. You just trot on the trout, and I'll eat any you don't want."

Tom was in a boastful mood. I cooked them all. Tom complained of fish-hunger after he had eaten his half of the last one.

It was a warm, sunny, lazy, comfortable afternoon. Our dishes were finished before three o'clock. We decided to cook the prunes, and while watching them to play a game of cribbage.

Not having had the advantages of Oriental nurture, we play cards in camp under certain disabilities. That is to say, we cannot squat, but must lean upon one elbow to play. Now I have a befuddled idea, probably incorrect, that the Romans banqueted in some such posture, and that indeed the whole Institution of the Divan rests—if you call it resting—upon the elbow. If that is true, the Divanic elbow must be acutely different from mine, for twenty-five minutes is the limit of my endurance. Then I must straighten up, if only for a moment.

On this afternoon, I must say, there was no opportunity for the elbow to become cramped. Tom laid out the ground-sheet; we began to play; immediately the mosquitoes arose and settled down upon us. In vain we puffed tobacco smoke at them. We did not consider ourselves justified in using our fly-dope to protect ourselves in the course of such a frivolous occupation as cribbage. If we did use that precious ointment now, and later the dreaded contingency of a dopeless long portage should arise, the pangs of guilty conscience would be unendurable. There was nothing for it but a smudge. Tom noted the direction of the wind and built a smudge, while I investigated and encouraged the simmering prunes. Then we settled down. Immediately the wind changed, and the smoke blew steadily and uselessly away from us, to the no small comfort of the mosquitoes. Not to be daunted by the feministic whim of a vagrant summer breeze, Tom built another smudge to fit its mood. Playfully, the merry little wanton shifted again, to the only quarter which could let both our smudgy exhalations drift away without helping us at all. While I kept the first two alive, Tom set up his third. Within the magic triangle—I had visions of a pentagon—we reclined in peace. The mosquitoes howled outside, while we in turn played, replenished the smudges, and wiped the tears from our smarting eyes. Whenever, in a momentary engrossment with the game, we allowed the smudge to grow languid or to lose its smudging virtue by blazing up too brightly, the mosquitoes would surge in like the legions of demons over the unguarded angle in a necromantic figure.

That evening, in the gathering dusk, we fished again. Tom stuck to his first post, and I naturally went back to the scene of my noonday triumphs. If I could get seven at noon, when everybody knows that fish do not bite, what could I not do at the fishing hour of eve! They seemed coy. In vain I dangled my Silver Doctors and Montreals before them. I tried the Dusty Miller, Par Belle, McGinty (since then by some ungrateful abuse of the deed poll misnamed the Western Bee), the Caddis Dark—all to no avail. I tried all I had. At last it was clear, even to me, that I could take no more trout from that spot on that day.

Even so, I might have continued casting until dark. There was a perfect purgation of all emotions in that secluded place, with its invitation to indolent reverie, its all-containing local self-sufficiency, its complete spiritual isolation from the world of men, its strange combining of intense absorption with free contemplation, its quiet delight for eye and ear and hand. There was a liberating monotony even in the mechanical, resignedly unhoping cast. The fever and the fret of life could find no culture medium to propagate their kind in that enchanted universe, as night closed down.

But the devil of it was that Tom was catching fish.

By the time I had worked round to him, he was taking his fifth trout off the hook. Hastily I replaced my flies with a worm. When, ten minutes later, we decided that it was too dark to fish any longer, he had six and I had two. A great content was on us both as we picked our way over the mass of logs and drift, and so to camp. We turned the frying-pan over the trout, stirred up the moribund fire, and thought of sitting outside for a short time. But the mosquitoes, which had succeeded the black flies as darkness fell, began to be troublesome again. The night took on a heavy quality, a hint of oppressiveness. There was no sense in trying to prolong the perfection of a day that was done. In about ten minutes we decided to go in.

Respectable tent-dwellers allow air to enter the tent at night. In the height of the fly season, this decent and hygienic custom can still be followed through the use of a mosquito-netting pinned across the open fly of the tent. But Tom and I are primitive and savage. Unable to appreciate the health-giving properties of fresh air, while on the other hand extremely well aware of the coarse and rude comfort of a pestless sleep, we close the tent as tightly as we can, and fill the space inside it with the foul reek of strong tobacco. We carry netting sufficient for the proper purpose thereof, but use it to seal the tent-fly, with the aid of half a dozen stout safety-pins. Boots, bacon and bundles are laid along the bottom of the wall, so that when we declare ourselves in for the night, our tent is as close to being airtight as we can arrange it to be. From the fact that the stale tobacco smoke has always disappeared before morning, I deduce that we swallow it in the course of the night, together with the fetid exhalations of the guttering candle-ends.

Nevertheless, our tent lives, like the lives of other savages, are governed by exact conventions. Tom always holds the flashlight while I spray the tent with flytox; immediately thereafter, the candle is always lighted. The broad-based, low, tin candlestick, found one afternoon long ago at a deserted northern camp-site, is always set up on the tackle-box at the back of the tent, between our heads, its rim held by the turned-down handle of the box. The bread is always on Tom's side; the medicine-case on mine, and the little haversack containing the flytox equipment, the candle-ends, and the mending kit. When we play our nightly game of cribbage, the white pegs are always Tom's, the red ones mine, except once or twice when he has demanded them, to change his luck.

We had not finished our preparations for bed when Tom noticed the first of our night sounds, a low, gentle, intermittent cluck, just outside the tent on his side. We gave up playing and listened. There was such a homely, domestic, housewifely quality to the sound that I felt like an intruder on a young mother's putting of her sleepy infant in its cot. Tom looked over at me, but I did not know what it was. Then, with a loudness and suddenness that startled us, another sound diverted our attention. Whip-poor-will! We were delighted for the first few minutes. We were patient for the first twenty-five minutes. Then we sought surcease from sorrow in our cribbage. When we had finished the rubber they were still at it, and my last waking impression was of a solitary call, perhaps the announcer signing off.

A RAINY DAY

CHAPTER V

It had been an uncomfortable sort of night, warm and sticky. I had wakened up but at last had gone to sleep again, after tossing and turning about for almost twenty minutes, I should judge. Then I had passed into a state of dreamy slumber, with all the soothing rhythms of the forest murmuring through my unconsciousness. The rhythms grew more insistent, and distant drums which had been muttering afar off came closer, with the tramp of steady feet upon a solid air. Just as I was growing dully resentful of the intrusions into our solitude, all the sounds ran together into the roar of an approaching train. I woke up, to hear the cosy sound of raindrops on the tent. It was more restful than sleep itself. Memories of summer nights of long ago came back—insufferable nights of steaming misery in a hot attic bedroom; the low mutter of distant thunder, and the sudden, cooling breeze; the amazing drop in temperature and the scurry to the shelter of discarded bed-clothes; then the quick gossip of clattering raindrops on the wooden shingles a few feet above, followed sometimes by the quiet, steady, gentle loquacity of a rain which has settled down to an all-night cradle song.

This happy, sentimental reverie was broken by a smart tap on my upturned nose. For the moment I did not recognize the source, but when I felt two more on my face I knew only too dismally what it was. The damned tent was leaking. Now a leaking tent by day is a disgusting companion, but since leaks are usually local, it is often possible to move out of their way both oneself and any parts of the equipment that one is anxious to keep dry. But a leaky tent at night is the foul fiend himself. At night every article has been carefully disposed, and may not be moved without annoyance. The blankets, which it is most desirable to keep dry, are spread out naked to the fury of the elements, once the elements get into the tent. One's clothing and matches and various minor perishables are more or less exposed. For a man trusts his tent, and if it proves a broken reed, he is indeed forlorn. A well-kept tent which goes leaky on its lord is a perfidious thing. Our tent was not old. I had once lent my old tent to a lady to camp a lake away. She returned it eventually, wrapped up as neatly as a Christmas parcel from a jewellery shop, so immaculate that I put it away unhesitatingly for the winter. Alas! when I opened it one day in the spring, I found that it was full within of ravening mildew. The lady had rolled it up carefully while it was still wet, with rain or with very heavy dew. Consequently, the tent of this present trip was not old and was not supposed to leak.

There is no conservatism more instinctive than that of the man—any man—who has just been wakened up at night. Any necessity for change, if it be only to get up and put on an extra blanket, is fiercely resented. Hence, I was irritated. I put a hand out in various directions to reach my treasures, my lares and penates. A little pool was forming in the hollow of my shirt. A soggy circle was spreading in my blanket. I felt for my hat. My hat is my nocturnal safe-deposit vault. I turn it upside down, and put in it my purse, my spectacles, my watch, my matches, my wallet with the travel permit, fishing licences and other state documents—and finally, my knife.

No knight ever cherished his sword, nor pioneer scout his gun, nor wife her wedding ring, nor boy his sling-shot, nor chorus girl her useful letters, nor bibliophile his first edition, nor chubby child her broken doll, with any more devotion than I cherish that knife. It is a clasp-knife, nine and five-eighths inches long, with a horn handle such as delighteth my soul. Its blade is four and a half inches, with a lovely, graceful, wicked curve to the back of it. That curve is the apple of my eye. It conveys the flattering suggestion that I go about killing bears and wolves and things, and that I would just as soon slit your weasand as look at you. It is my consolation for a boyhood wasted, far from the bloody glories of the Jolly Roger. The steel is somewhat soft.

Two gnawing fears chew at my vitals. Some day I shall lose that knife; I know it. Or else some day the precious cradle into which my blade snaps when not in use will be browned with rust. I guard against this latter contingency by washing the knife with extreme and personal care. I never dip the whole knife into water. I always wash the handle with the back upward.

I felt in my hat. It was dry. I touched the knife, at the moment when a large drop fell upon it. It had to be lying face up, of course, and the recess for the blade was a miniature water-trough. As one result of this discovery, Tom woke up. Then I switched on the flashlight. On

Tom's side the rain was dripping from the bottom of a careless wrinkle; on mine it was dropping briskly from a seam. Why I had put my hat under this particular seam, I do not know. The hat was not in its proper place, and I was paying the penalty for an outraged convention. Tom moved the bread and his trousers from beneath the wrinkle; I shifted my hat and my shirt—in fact, I took my shirt under the blanket to dry it. I wiped my knife assiduously for ten minutes. I moved my head. By the time all these measures had been taken the leaking had ceased. The tightening of the wet tent-ropes had removed the wrinkle, and my seam, having filled up, was now doing its water-shedding duty.

When we woke up in the morning, it was still raining, though not very hard. We had, of course, neglected to lay in any kindling. Generally, if we have made camp early enough to provide it, we have a little birch bark, and a few slivers of fat pine, which we inaccurately call pitch pine, tucked away at the foot of the tent when we turn in. Even in clear weather a fire can be lighted more quickly with dry kindling than with wood which has been drenched in dew, and in the matter of the morning fire, time is very important. A noon fire also seems to me to call for haste, but an afternoon or evening fire may be quite slow without arousing any resentment in me. In the morning, however, the sight of some bone-dry yellow slivers of pine and a sheet of birch bark is exceeding welcome.

If it had been noon, we could have eaten a cold lunch in the tent—bread and butter, some cheese, a quartered onion, chipped beef perhaps, and a spoonful of jam. A hearty and a pleasant meal that, with a picnic tang to it. But a cold breakfast is a dreary meal. The chilled innards call for hot tea: in addition, Tom's call for toast; mine for porridge. Moreover, we had the evening's catch of trout. These must be cooked at once. So fastidious does one become in the matter of fresh fish in the bush that trout kept uncooked past one meal are regarded as scarcely fit for human consumption. The butter may be rancid, and the bread mouldy; no matter. But we sniff at fish kept over night, even with frost in the air; and there was no frost in the air.

Fire-lighting in the rain is, however, no real problem in the Park, unless there has been a long spell of wet weather. Kindling the fire is a slower process than in dry times, and sticks must be split that otherwise would burn in the round, but there is usually birch not far off, and a pine stump somewhere near. With these, one can light a fire and soon have it burning briskly in a teeming rain. Once the initial discomfort of leaving the dry tent is past, there is nothing to a rainy morning, if one does not have to break camp. That is different.

We cooked and ate our breakfast, and washed the dishes. Tom dried them, and turned them upside down on a log. Then we suddenly felt wet and forlorn, and dashed for the shelter of the tent. Perhaps it was because the dishes washed, we had let the fire die down, and immediately found ourselves out in the rain.

I had had the day all planned. There was still a mile of portage. The trail—a pleasant, needle-strewn path, wide and happy for all but the last hundred yards, which dropped abruptly down a slippery bank—led to an ancient, broken dam at the lower end of little Lake Lavague. The old dam itself has such trouty-looking water below it that I have never been able to rid myself of the hope of decent fishing there, although, to tell the truth, I have never yet caught anything. It seemed to me that there must be good trout holes in the wild stretch of turbulence between the old dam and the Forks, and I had proposed that we walk up the trail to the old dam and fish the stream back down to the Forks. Tom, ready for anything, had been quite enchanted with the idea.

Once inside the tent, we found it hot and stuffy. The thought of a whole day's cribbage, enticing a few minutes before, grew more and more distasteful. Playing cards seemed a footling way for healthy men to spend a day. Tom lit a cigarette.

"I suppose it's too wet to fish this morning," he said.

"It's pretty wet," I replied gloomily.

"I guess they wouldn't bite."

"Well, I don't know."

"Kind of a warm rain."

"Why, do you want to try it anyway?" I asked, half-hopefully.

"I'd just as soon," said Tom. "What time is it?"

It was just after eight. Our minds made up, we set to work gaily to get the tackle ready. Once on the trail and with our feet thoroughly soaked, we actually grew hilarious. Huge bracken rose up and splashed us; tall timothy, left behind seventy years before when the tote-teams plodded along the newly-built lumbering road, drenched our knees: but all was in fun, in friendly horse-play, so to speak.

In the rain, and unburdened, one does not note the details of a trail, especially if it is a familiar one. Tom, following for the first time, may have been observant, but I was not. As a result, I was surprised when the sudden roar of water told me we must be near the old dam. A minute or two afterwards we began to descend the slippery, spring-moistened clay of that last drop to the Creek level. Between a timbered wing of the dam and a long, mossy, half-rotted log, the trail ends on a narrow strip of sand, perhaps two hundred yards from the lower end of tiny Lavague.

Of course we tried the water just below the dam, picking our way very daintily over the criss-crossed, crumbling structure to the boulders and rocks below. It appeared perfect for trout, with its swirls, its quiet, steady side-runs, its pools and rock-chambered recesses. But there was no sign of fish. Tom soon gave up and called to me that he was going to a high rock farther down, that seemed to cut the Creek abruptly off. I watched him pick his way along the boulders near the shore, saw him climb once up the bank to avoid a birch that lay out over the Creek, not more than eighteen inches above the water, saw him come down again and swing precariously under another small tree that bent beneath his weight. When I saw him perched on a smaller neighbour of the big rock, I resolved to follow.

Since I should be trying below the big rock, I decided not to work along the shore, but to go part way up the bank and push through the underbrush. There were faint traces of a trail, probably made by the river-drivers. This ghost of a trail was not really worse than no trail at all; it only seemed so because of the false hopes it raised. Now I have never yet learned the wisdom of taking down a line for a fifty yard scramble through undergrowth. Hence, I continue to go madly on my twisting, tearing, disentangling, breaking, imprecating way, backing up, turning round, ducking under twigs, crawling under and over logs, and eventually arriving at the wrong place. No one who has never tried it will realize the exasperating difficulty there can be in fifteen feet of low growth, especially that growth which immediately overhangs a small unkempt stream in wooded Ontario. Passage parallel to such a stream is bad enough, but direct ascent from, or descent to it is indescribable. A hundred times that morning we were forced to make our way through such growth; rarely could we move more than fifty or sixty yards along the boulders by the water. The far shore always appeared ridiculously free for passage, but we could never cross.

We had thus painfully and fruitlessly worked down three-quarters of the distance to the Forks. Tom had caught four, but only one large enough to keep; I had taken three, all of them too small. I had slid off stones and sprained an ankle; I had scraped a large area of skin off my leg; I had torn my trousers. We were, of course, wet through from head to foot. Both of us were in a state of almost constant anxiety, but especially Tom. A good bit of the time we were out of sight of each other. Since almost every other step involved grave danger of a broken leg, in these remote parts only slightly less disastrous than a broken neck, each of us, especially Tom, imagined the other in some horrible situation whenever the other lingered longer than usual out of sight. Both of us have more confidence in Tom than Tom has in me. He holds a conviction, which he fondly believes is a secret, that I am clumsy and slow in motor co-ordination, as well as up in years. I am. Nevertheless, we were keenly enjoying the day.

We had had one adventure. I was trying a likely spot on one of the irregular arcs made by a bend in the stream. Tom had seen a tempting pool some thirty yards or so farther along, and made his way towards it. After having passed some remark as he went by, I paid no further immediate attention to him until I looked up quickly at the sound of a sharp yell. Tom was watching something on the shore, and there was a hint in his tense immobility of more than common interest. He called again, but without even turning toward me. All excited now, I flipped my rod back, landing my hooks well up a tall cedar, and hurried round to him. As I stumbled and climbed and slithered, I saw him back up a step, stoop over, reach to one side, and without turning his head, pick up a heavy piece of wood.

"Hey, are you coming? There's two of 'em!" he shouted.
"Yes. What?" I shouted back.
"I don't know."

Then I heard a low, menacing noise, half-way between a spit and a growl. Tom backed up another step and raised his weapon. I was almost beside him before I saw it—a savage, lifted head, not much larger than a heavy cat's, on the near end of a brown creature of low but stocky build, about two feet long. Almost at once I saw the other one of the pair, a few inches behind the first, but equally unpleasant to look at. They would be twelve feet away, when I reached Tom. Almost immediately afterwards they were eleven feet away, and the one behind had pulled up beside the other.

I didn't like the situation. It was fun, in a way, and it was undeniably thrilling, but it was too uncertain. I judged them to be martens, and I suspected that young Marten near by had a headache or something and was not to be disturbed. Moreover, I have had comparatively little experience at fighting martens, and did not know the rules. Although it was two to two, there was not another stick available, and this left us at a disadvantage. Even though I had my trusty knife, which of course I drew, somehow or other those two creatures wore an air of recklessness that threatened rapid and decisive strokes before I could swing into action, with my sluggish motor responses. I knew that we could dispose of them eventually, but with much attendant and consequent and maybe permanent discomfort. They spat and snarled again, and moved six inches closer, in perfect concert.

"Maybe we oughtn't to tease the poor brutes," I suggested. "If we try to pass them, they'll think we're trying to get their young or something. Say we go back."

"Okay. I don't like the look of them anyway," said honest Tom. "What are they?"

So we backed away from them. They stood still, without a further sound, and watched us. Then suddenly, silently, they were not there. Tom dropped his club and I folded my knife again. It is against the law to kill fur-bearing animals in the Park at any time. We made a wide circuit round them, so as not to disturb the suffering infant, and watched and listened carefully. But not any sign did we see or hear of the two that had so undauntedly confronted us.

As I said, we were now fully three-quarters of the way down, though at the time we had no means of judging that with any degree of assurance. The little valley was much wider, and there were long stretches that had been timbered to guide the logs along the channel. From one of these, too straight to promise much fishing, we had turned well up the bank and followed along in reasonable comfort for two or three hundred yards. When we descended again, we found ourselves in the most interesting bit we had yet seen above the Forks. The south bank, our bank, here closely hugged by the stream, was quite high. A large half-moon valley, littered with boulders and drift, revealed the width of the Creek in the wild, mad days of the spring break-up. Just where we came down, a huge pine had some day fallen across the stream, carrying before it an only slightly smaller companion. Later, a third had been lodged across them by some unusually high water. The three bridged the stream ten feet above the present level of the Creek.

Standing on this bridge, Tom dropped a fly—he was using flies today—and almost instantaneously had a strike that nearly toppled him off his log. There was no room for two at this point, but at the upper end of the bow, a hundred yards away, was a perfect pool. I had been fishing in vain all morning in perfect pools, but this was different. I was now for the first time on the north side of the Creek. I had been seeing, all along, ideal fishing spots just out of reach on the north side, and I had developed the stubborn conviction that on the north side the trout barely had finning room, and were all lined up, half-famished, in a piscine bread-line. Here I was at last on the magic side, and I fairly ran in my eagerness to reach the place.

There is a special thrill in exploring new fishing grounds. One little fellow—legal size, of course—taken from a virgin spot, is worth half a dozen beauties from the teeming Lavieille Dam. There has been the proof derived from close examination or from swift, ecstatic, unreasoning intuition that trout must be here if trout exist anywhere. There is the tingling cast, the lightning strike which confirms for ever a man's faith in his own judgment and obliterates the memory of more than threescore failures.

I was breathless. I was afraid to cast. It would be too heartbreaking to fail here. I heard faintly Tom's triumphant shout. Then I cast, and almost at the same moment I too yelled. Ten minutes afterwards, my trout safely landed, I started towards Tom. He was on his way to me, proudly holding up a fish of practically the same size as mine, which means, I suppose, a little bigger. I do not remember the actual dimensions of those two trout, but they were larger than anything we had caught the day before, and we were jubilant. We tried again each in his own place; we changed places; but we caught nothing more. Nor did we get anything the rest of the way down. Not that it mattered. We were content, and more than content. When we saw the big rock which marked the actual Forks, the fishing hole of yesterday, and turned up to the trail, now close to the stream, we suddenly became conscious that it was still raining, had been raining all the time. We were fiercely hungry. It was nearly two o'clock.

That afternoon, clad in dry socks and the woollen combinations that we used for night wear, we played cribbage, in a vast atmosphere of satisfaction, as we retraced, in unwearying detail, all the joyous process which I insisted upon describing as "whipping the stream." About half-past five it faired up, and we fished again, but without very great success. We did get two or three with worms, which Tom was now beginning to scorn with a fine but ungrateful scorn. Indeed, in the exuberance of the afternoon's reminiscences, he had proposed turning the worms loose, as bait scarce fit for real trout fishermen. The evening's experience reconciled him, however, to the lowliness of worms again. 'Tis better to have caught with worms than never to have caught at all.

We had kept the fire going, in order to dry our clothes, and we came in early to complete the drying process. It consisted in piecemeal steaming and partial burning of the clothing and ourselves by means of various contortional positions near the fire. The moon came up and flooded our little clearing with brilliance, and the temperature went down and chilled whatever parts of us were away from the flame. We crowded as close to it as possible, and were prodigal with wood, and smoked and shivered, reluctant to go in. But to enjoy the moonlight we must let the fire die down, and to keep warm we must feed the fire. At last we gave up.

Inside the tent, we itched intolerably. Only now did we realize how ferociously the black-flies and mosquitoes had attacked us. We were provided with netting, which protected our faces and necks quite well, when we used it. But who can keep a face-net on when he is fishing? Moreover, the attempt to get at the tormentors always leaves gaps through which fresh hordes of foes press forward to the assault. In addition to the customary bloody places behind the ears, there are well-defined lines of scars wherever a garment ends or buttons. Each of us had a horrible itching line up the front of his body, two red cuff-lines at the bottoms of his sleeves and at the tops of his socks, as well as a broad bleeding belt around his waist. At times of change from day wear to night wear these areas are most distressful. Each year I swear that I shall come next season in a one-piece garment, or at the least I shall zipper everything that will zip. But when the next year comes along I have forgotten the misery.

It was cold in the tent. Having had our cribbage in the afternoon, we did not care to play again, with the indirect consequence that the tent was not candle-heated to begin the night. Tom announced that he was going to wear a sweater in addition to his woollens. At my suggestion, and after my example, he also put his breeks back on. Why we wore breeks in the bush in those old, far-off but not unhappy days, I do not know. The breeks were responsible for the annual garters of black-fly bites, as well as for other inconveniences. I put on both my pairs of heavy woollen socks, and a shirt. At approximately two o'clock, I put on my Hudson's Bay mackinaw. Occasionally I could hear Tom fumbling about, and knew that he was gradually heaping up all that would remain heaped over him. At four o'clock I emptied my hat and put it on, together with my gloves. At long last the time came to get up. I looked over at Tom. As usual, he was utterly hidden, with his blanket pulled completely over his head, and the bag of bread topping the heap of which he was the core. I lay still a while, until I saw a patch of light on the tent. It was so cheery and yellow that I was emboldened to risk the frigid world, and with chattering teeth I crawled out of my bedding. Since I had to take my night woollens off, I had less on when I was dressed than when I had been in bed, but five minutes sufficed to start a brisk, crackling fire, and under its genial heat my stiff, cramped joints were loosened, and the general shrinking in upon myself of all those weary hours was over. There had been quite a heavy frost, and I had to break ice in a billy that had been left overnight with water in it. When the water for the tea and for the porridge was close to boiling, I went over to the tent and called Tom. There was a squirming under that incongruous mess, and the bag of bread rolled off. A confused murmur, and with a mighty heave of bedding, Tom arose. I took one amazed look and howled with laughter. Tom had two sweaters, one a very heavy red garment, the other a delicate blue creation. He was wearing the blue in a conventional manner, the red not so, for his feet protruded from its sleeves. Tom had a sweater on at each end.

This was the morning on which I suspected him of not having the root of the matter in him. Just after breakfast we saw the five moose feeding near the lily-pads among which we had seen them the first morning after our arrival at the Forks. This decided us to take the morning off, in order to paddle up the marshy indolence of the White

Partridge far enough to see what lay beyond the wooded point which cut off our view of it. In the afternoon we would fish down the gloomy gorges between the Forks and the lower end of the long portage up which we had come that nightmare afternoon. There was no hurry. I had put the beans to soak the night before, and we began cooking them as soon as a cooking billy was free. I saw Tom look at me and rub his face meditatively.

"Going to shave today?" he asked.

I was genuinely shocked, and said I was. During all my camping life I had been looking for the noble savage, the man who could accept all his privileges, including the abandonment of razor and comb. I had never found one. Dear friends who had boasted of their kinship with the brutes, who had even gone so far as to yell a savage yell and cut a primitive caper, I had caught surreptitiously using a pocket comb or even blatantly setting the stage for a full shaving operation. Their excuse had always been the same poor paltry plea that they could not endure the discomfort of an unshaven countenance. Their miserable hypocrisy was ridiculously easy to expose, for the necks they were about to shave were raw with black-fly bites and swollen with mosquito ravages, and their protesting hands were patterned with bramble scratches and furrowed by fishhook gougings. And they talked about the discomfort of an unshaved face! Not a bit of it: the explanation was purely atavistic; they were reverting to their shaven type. In such cases, the will to effeteness is stronger than the will to naturalness; they always shaved, and of course I had to do so, since I was always tacitly in the rôle of partial guest or partial host, and either one imposed the obligation of conformity in a matter like this. But I had had better hopes of Tom. He had seemed closer to Nature's great beating heart—and things of that sort. I told him all that, and he put the thought away. He shaved the next morning, however, without consulting me.

We paddled a lazy two hours up the languid White Partridge, creeping quite close to a moose and calf, getting in between a fawn and its mother, trying unsuccessfully to paddle near enough a beautiful deer to take a snapshot, watching a brood of ducks which contained one heedless duckling, with an over-anxious mother, too obviously concerned to entice us into pursuit of her. At one place we startled seven deer, heard the rough whistle, and from seven spots, four of them unsuspected, saw the white tails go up and the hindquarters rise as the herd plunged out of the marsh and into the protecting invisibility of the wooded hills. Once we outlasted a deer in patience, remaining still so long that the lifted head was lowered again and the feeding was resumed. It was a restful, warm and busy morning, with animated nature as purveyor of business and with us as spectators.

The afternoon was neither so restful nor so animated. As I said, we had decided to fish down from the Forks. Through extremely narrow, deep, dark gorges the Creek cuts its fierce way, its drop so uninterrupted that not for two and a half miles is there a moment of placidity, its rocky shore so precipitous and wild and high that only for short intervals could we follow beside the water. Fortunately, the trail ran fairly close to it almost all the way. There seemed so many lurking-places, in the sheltering bits beneath great boulders around which foaming cataracts plunged, that we dreamed of monster trout, and were disappointed when three little nine-inch fellows and half a dozen throw-backs made up our total. Still, the clambering and the expectancy and the dark romantic beauty sufficed for our demands. That evening, however, as we washed the dishes, we knew that the time had come to leave the Forks. Once that was agreed upon, and all the agreeing had been done before either of us mentioned the subject, we were so anxious to be gone that we carried the canoe up the trail to the old dam, to lighten the next day's labour. Even then, we were back in time to take out half a dozen beauties at the meeting of the waters, in a quiet, golden sunset and a dusk so inviting we grew loath to leave.

THE ROCK CAMP

CHAPTER VI

WE WERE up bright and early next morning, and at work on our packing. The tent was too wet with dew to permit taking down, but there was a good deal we could putter at. It promised to be a sunny day, clear and quiet. I was anxious to get on our way, especially since I was uncertain as to some of the details of the route. Our destination for the day was Lavieille Dam, which really marked the beginning of Lake Lavieille. The distance was not great, not more than five or six miles, I suppose, but we had a couple of mile carries and an indefinite number of short portages, lifts, pulls and awkward bits of water. All in all, it would be rough going. Moreover, I knew a spot just at the foot of the Dam, and I wanted to be there in time to drop in a line before sunset. The mosquitoes were, if possible, worse than they had been on any previous day. At last the dishes were all washed, the packs done up, and we had only to wait until the tent should be dry enough to move. We had kept the fire burning to provide a smoke against the mosquitoes. I took down my rod while Tom shaved.

He built up a small portable smudge on a rusty old piece of tin he had found.

"I'll be back in a minute," he said, as he started off into the bush with his smudge.

It was nearly nine o'clock when we finally set out. We crossed the unsteady mass of driftwood piled up above the sluice, paused to bid a regretful farewell to the Forks, stopped some fifty yards beyond for a last cool drink from the little run of spring water that trickled across the trail, its flow so shallow we must wait for the sediment to settle after each dipping in of the cup, even with a scooped-out microscopic pool as a reservoir. We tramped happily along the unimpeded, grass-grown way; passed the open place that seemed so metropolitan and busy, even though a bird was the only sign of activity, the place at which the White Partridge trail branches off to the left; passed the broken twig by which we had marked the point immediately above the good fishing spot in the Creek; tried in vain to take a picture of a mother partridge, with the wing so pitifully and so cunningly injured, which had attempted by means of that worn old trick to lead us away from the young brood, too old now to keep motionless under leaves. We climbed over the huge, barkless, crumbling pine that must have crashed across our trail half a century before.

Tom kept a sharp look-out for spruce gum. It appears that he has an inequitable agreement with half the children in his town to supply them with enormous quantities of spruce gum. Accordingly, all his waking moments on the trail, and many of his leisure moments in camp, are burdened with the necessity of finding gum-covered spruces. Tom would rather find a superlatively productive sprucegum tree than free gold. He uses an exasperating amount of time in this occupation, and as far as I can learn, the only requital he obtains is the innocent and wholly charming satisfaction he derives from an occasional substitution of pine pitch, a very adhesive and turpentinish substance, for the stipulated spruce gum. I am given to understand that he extracts great enjoyment from the prolonged facial contortions of his astonished little friends at these times.

Arrived at the old dam, we could not resist the blandishments of the place, and wasted half an hour. Tom investigated the point of embarkation, and admitted a strong distaste for it. In the first place, it was much too close to the dam, toward which and over which the water was flowing with considerable velocity. In the second place, there were rocks. We'd be in a pretty mess if we put into the water here and found ourselves within ten or fifteen seconds trying to flounder ashore, with a canoe all smashed into wet kindling, and not even any matches left to light this kindling to cook the food we should no longer have. His picture was too disturbing, and we carried everything up through a malignant maze of fallen timber, brambles, and undergrowth to where the Creek widened into the lake.

I doubt if the lake is half a mile wide. There is nothing very remarkable about its irregularly rounded shape, its rather low, generally marshy shore, or in the character of the tree-growths surrounding it, but there is a shy remoteness, a quality of solitariness, which Tom and I find appealing.

Little Lake Lavague separates two worlds. The world from which we had just come had not been burned over, and the trail, bedded deep in humus and leaves and needles, had led us through a full growth of mixed hardwood and conifers, a broad and easy way which carried the restful atmosphere of a long period of undisturbed tranquillity.

THE INCOMPLETE ANGLERS

The world into which we entered when we crossed Lavague was very different. It had been swept by fire not very many years before, and then not for the first time in this cosmic epoch. What growth there was consisted of small poplars, with a few birches scattered through them. Nothing was more than twenty or twenty-five feet high, and there was no protection from the blazing sun. Except in low places, a great deal of the humus had been burnt off, leaving the sand to be washed from the narrow ridge along which the trail ran. As a consequence, much of the going was over bare and sloping rock. Gaunt rampikes; blackened stumps; long slim spidery trees, leafless, but with all branches still on them, fallen through lack of soil for their roots, yet sustained horizontally in mid-air by the limbs underneath, in a horrible kind of dead processional; thick bramble tangles; brilliant fireweed; bracken and mosses—these made up the chief features of the landscape. It seemed the very abomination of desolation, yet it held a beauty and a fascination that were not macabre.

At the beginning of this trail—a low, wet beginning, too—there was on the right side as we came up from the lake a weather-beaten drying-rack and a decrepit stone fireplace with blackened little buns of charred wood underneath, while on the left two upturned, blackened stumps oozed misery. For me, the whole scene at that moment suggested only the exhausted lethargy left in the wake of a destructive activity. It suggested nothing of the kind to Tom. While I was lashing the poles for the carry, he had slipped round the stumps to investigate, and had seen, not a hundred yards away, what he maintains was a gigantic bull moose. I accepted the identification, but have up to this time of writing refused Tom's estimate of size. Judging from his account, the thing must have been a mastodon.

It was gone, of course, before Tom could get back and call me to see it, but for him it cast a ruddy glow of majestic vitality over that lifeless scene.

The portage was only fifteen minutes, but the last five minutes' carrying was by far the worst we had had, since it involved clambering steeply over irregular rock which would not accommodate itself to the angles required for comfortable movement, which insisted upon piling itself up in ridges, with troughs between so narrow that the front end of the canoe was likely to bump against the next mass immediately after the rear end had bounced back from the mass behind. Before this bit began, the trail had passed imperceptibly over a smooth table of bare rock just where trail and Creek rejoin each other, after a businesslike short cut by the former. Returning empty from the first trip, we resolved to lunch here on the way back with the second load. It was nearly twelve.

The Creek follows a rugged course hereabouts, so rugged and formidable, in fact, that extensive timbering up had been done in the old logging days. When he came up with the water for the tea and dishes, Tom reported his positive conviction that trout lay hidden within those brown depths. But, uncertain as to the length of time we should require to reach the big Dam, and anxious to do our evening fishing there, I was reluctant to spare the hour or more that we were bound to waste if we tried here. Besides, the tackle was at the end of the trail, and all packed up. Tom did not press the matter, and after lunch we washed the dishes, packed up the stuff, and bade the place farewell.

We noted a tantalizing profusion of perfect fishing spots along that rough bit at the end. A couple of bait-boxes and some emptied tin cans, one of which had contained sardines, indicated previous parties that had not hurried on. A firm belief of ours is that all those who have fished previously where we fish have had incredibly good luck. By the time we pushed the canoe off I was as sure as Tom that we were leaving behind us the best fishing grounds of the whole expedition. It seemed to me, too, that the portage, rough as it was, might with propriety have been extended another fifty yards. The water moved too swiftly for comfort towards that series of intimidating plunges beside and beyond our luncheon site. We kept close to the shore, and, to avoid the mid-current perils, we crept below overhanging trees so little above the water that we had to lift their branches in order to pass. Then we reached a stretch of quiet where the stream flowed over golden ripples of sand—a stretch that appeared to Tom to teem with menace. We had barely entered it when he stopped paddling, turned round and said,

"What kind of time do you think we've made today?"

"Fine," I replied. "A good deal better than I figured on."

I was amazed at his next remark.

"You know, I've kind of got the bug. It strikes me maybe we're leaving the best place behind on the whole Creek. Would it take too long to go back there and just drop a line?"

In spite of my earlier objection, I knew there was plenty of time to do it. I dislike turning back when I have once set out, and I disliked the labour of climbing up that current again. But we turned back.

Almost immediately we wished we had not. I should have remembered from the Petawawa experience on our first day that it is much more nerve-racking to go down a swift water than up. A few yards above the portage we struck something which seemed to lift up one side of the canoe. The tip was very slight, but it was enough. I had one clear, astonished moment of premonition, without any impulse to do anything; then I was floundering and gasping and grappling in the cold, fiercely pulling water. It came very little above my waist, but in that current I had real difficulty in keeping up against it. We both grasped at the canoe, and I caught the bag of bread just as it was darting past me. We were not more than eight or ten feet from the nearer bank, and before I was very sure of what had happened, we had the canoe on the boulder-strewn shore. Two or three of the bundles were setting off, but as they had all been thrown well towards the land, and most of them had not fallen out of the canoe at all, we caught the strays without much difficulty, except that Tom almost lost his beaver log. We dragged the bundle containing the tent and the blankets up beside the canoe; then we sat down and stared at each other.

It was not very funny, but there seemed little to do at the moment except to laugh. We were both so relieved to be ashore, and with an undamaged craft, that there was no room for exasperation. We emptied the water out of the two cameras and the tackle-box, turned the canoe over and lifted it well away from the edge of the stream. Then we carried all that sodden mass back over the trail to the bare rock table on which we had lunched. There was no possible place nearer the end of the portage.

Disconsolately we opened up all our containers and spread everything out on the rock. Luckily, the sun was shining hot. Our sugar we could not spread out; it was too syrupy. The flour was dry. The tea, about which we worried least, was soaked, and to judge by its insipidity during the rest of the trip it was also semi-steeped. Some of the oatmeal was in lumps, and the bread was a bit doughy in places. Tom's fine-cut tobacco had lost much of its savour. The matches, to our consternation, were fairly swimming. We laid them all out, carefully and individually separated, and watched them with solicitude. Our anxiety was needless, for once dry, they were quite as serviceable as before. The cameras tended later to become unglued. The films they contained were ruined, but our unused stock had not been harmed. Even our night-wear was dry, or almost dry, and we scampered about in it while we dried the rest of our clothing. Our state documents had been carefully wrapped in oiled silk, and were quite uninjured. The playing cards were sticking together, and in the process of separating them we left two or three identifying adhesions which we afterwards affected to ignore. Hitherto our white and red cribbage pegs had been kept indifferently in the two holes made in each end of the board. But when, with some difficulty, we now dug out the pegs, we found that the colour in the red ones had run and dyed their nests. This circumstance gave them permanent possession of the reddened end and still serves pleasantly to remind us of that complete immersion, each time we play. A merry little breeze sprang up, scattering our precious matches among the bushes and mosses and down the crevices. Then it died down again.

For a time we were too much worried over the extent of the damage done to enjoy the situation, and were ourselves too uncomfortable. But as the blankets began to steam and dry, and especially when the first timidly struck match burst into flame, we came to see the fun of it, after we had finished gathering up again the scattered matches. Then we grew hungry, and ate gluttonously, though it was scarcely five o'clock.

We had abandoned any thought of going farther that

day, but we were not greatly troubled. Much of the satisfaction in our method of camping arises from our refusal to set down a rigid schedule. If we wish to alter our tentative plans, or are compelled to do so, we can make changes without any sense of defeat. We had recognized at once that we were here for the night, and had selected the best available tent-site, a sorry one on this rock-ribbed coast.

Our drying duties had left us no time for fishing until late, and for local reasons night came before its time. Our side of the Creek was fairly flat and low, but on the other side a high bank, heavily wooded with spruce and pine, rose abruptly from the water and towered above us, showing a serrated skyline behind which the sun sank early in the evening. Before it sank, however, it had completed its task for us, and once more we were in comfort.

The night tempted us to sit outside by the fire. No one camped here regularly, and wood was easy to come by. At the Forks, because the many May fishing parties, in from White Partridge way and Lake Traverse, used up the fire-wood close at hand, it was necessary for June campers to go some distance for good wood. At the Forks, too, although we had a delightfully open space for the camp-site itself, the forest crowded up close around us and shut off most of the sky. Here, we found a liberating spaciousness. With the coming of the dark, the dreary traces of fire ceased to be in evidence. To the south, east and north-east, the star-bright expanse of the heavens sparkled over us. The moon was not to rise until after ten. To the west and north-west the sombre curve of the great black hills gave us a skyline that glinted and became alive in the sharp contrast between deep black woods and vibrant sky. The north pulsated faintly with what we thought might turn out to be the northern lights. Thirty yards away the Creek kept up its low, conversational roar. An owl hooted two or three times.

We sat and smoked in silence.

> *I saw eternity the other night,*
> *Like a great ring of pure and endless light,*
> *All calm, as it was bright.*

At last, through the pines far to the south-east, a yellow clown came laughing up. The jesting moon, low in the eastern sky, has done much to counteract the mischief caused by its own romantic aspects. The sane Greeks did not have their frivolous gods for nothing. We watched it until it had extricated itself from the meshes of foliage, and with gathering dignity rode clear. Then, with a sigh, I stood up and stretched myself. We separated the embers and beat out the fire with sticks. Tom slipped down to the Creek for water.

We knew that the night would be cold, but with half a dozen blanket pins each of us managed to improvise a fair substitute for a sleeping-bag. We were less troubled over the prospective cold than over the utter lack of downiness in our beds. We are in general rather careless about our mattresses. We know how to make, and have on occasion made, very fragrant and springy balsam beds. We also know how to make up a good couch of bracken. But when we have only two or three weeks altogether, it seems foolish to waste any of that precious time in such an unprofitable occupation, or at any rate to waste as much time as would be required if we accustomed ourselves to expecting such softness. Once in a while we take possession of a second-hand balsam or bracken bed if we find it exactly where we wish to pitch our tent. If it is balsam, we have always entered into possession so long after the building that the boughs are dead, and the enervating voluptuousness a thing of the past. We have discussed patent inflatable beds, and when once we saw a number advertised as seconds at a very reasonable price, we almost considered buying them. Normally, what we have beneath us at night is a ground-sheet for protection against the dampness, with one thickness of a blanket for mattress.

After the second night, one craves no more—and this was our fifth night. Nevertheless, our willingness to sit out by the fire had been reinforced by a lack of enthusiasm for our prospective beds. It is one thing to lie on resilient grass, or a layer of humus, or porous sand or soft clay; it is quite another to stretch out on uneven, solid rock. To be sure, we had soil under part of the bed-space, but we knew we must literally endure hardness.

I had nicely crawled into my pinned-up sleeping-bag before I realized that there was a small, somewhat pointed stone embedded in my part of the soil area, just about where my lumbar region should have rested, but could not. I was unwilling to disarrange my completed retirement for one little stone, and tried to move away from it. I could do this, but so diabolically situated was it that as soon as my vigilance was relaxed through drowsiness I rolled exactly upon it. I finally gave up the effort to avoid it and squirmed round and out enough to reach my tormentor, cursing myself for not having done so before. It was so difficult to get at, and so surprisingly tenacious of its position, that I was forced to come still farther out. I grubbed around that stone, no longer small. It was a stone apart. I knew that, for I could wiggle it slightly. At last, I abandoned the attempt to clear away the obstruction to my peace while remaining in bed, and emerged. I scratched madly at the ground, like a dog burrowing under a root. I had not imagined there was as much soil in the whole district as I was throwing up around me. The stone grew larger as it went down and down. Suddenly there was the crackle and the flash of a match.

"Hey, what are you doing? Burying a bone?" Tom called out.

Then he roared with ill-timed laughter. I was undoubtedly a sight, but I was in no mood to appreciate merriment. I thought it abominably ungrateful, because for half a moment I almost persuaded myself that I had deliberately taken this side of the bed to spare him the stone. Actually, of course, I was on the side which custom assigned to me; custom as set up by myself the first night of the trip. However, I said nothing to him, even when he switched on the flashlight. By that time I was down about a foot, and the boulder was uncovered, a great brute of a pyramid that could not hold its own against my seething wrath when its earthy protection had been removed. I heaved it up, flung aside my carefully piled dunnage, raised the tent-wall opposite, and rolled the damned thing outside. The rest of the night I spent settling into and crawling out of the hole into which the stone had fitted.

Morning comes, even after the most uncomfortable of nights, with its amazing discovery in the woods that after all one has had adequate rest, and feels refreshed and ready for the day. We had decided to have a fairly early breakfast. When I turned the frying-pan over the fireplace in token that the dishes were done, even to the pots and pans, it was five minutes to seven. We had set up the rods the night before, and were ready.

As usual, there were some holes which seemed perfect to us, but which had no interest at all for trout. Just below our camp was one of these. The water poured down in a heavy, sullen, brown sheet to an enormous pot, and escaped from one small break in the rim. Across this pot lay a gigantic pine, from which a man could cast to any part of the caldron. But not a trout rose. We worked our way down the stream, trying each likely place, but we had passed the dramatic part, and the Creek had simmered down to a playful little brook that brightly chased its tail round shallow eddies and dimpled its straw-coloured and transparent course over inconsequential shelves in the most pastoral manner imaginable, before we had a strike. It was Tom's, and I had to watch him lift out and hold up proudly for inspection the best trout we had taken. Idling, absentmindedly trying to cast into a special globule of light on the farther side of the current, I felt a strike so powerful that I forgot all elementary instruction and jerked —out into the empty air, of course. Then I settled down to retrieve that silly error. Over and over again I cast to that globule; I cast above it and let my flies drift past; I cast below it and pulled up through it; I changed my flies. I tried below and caught a good one, which I almost—but not quite—threw back in disgust. Tom had taken two more, and called to me to come over to his spot. He had lost a beauty. Still I cast, against all experience, which told me I might as well expect to hook a mermaid as that trout now. But fortune is a fickle jade and trout are kittle cattle. In the same globule it struck again. This time I had it hooked. During the last fifteen of the twenty-five minutes I required to land that trout, Tom was a spectator. He had watched me for a while; then, realizing that this was no everyday event, he had come back to me. I was glad he was there. The first few times I had caught a glimpse of my trout I had determined to land it myself, but by the end of twenty minutes I was no longer haughty about it. So when Tom offered to net it for me I accepted gratefully.

We have since taken larger speckled trout from the lakes, but that remains the biggest from the Creek itself. We called it Grandpa. An acute sense of relativity in these matters, and a fear that anglers in more tremendous waters might smile at our superlative for Grandpa, prevent my giving the actual dimensions of our prize. We have them, both in length and girth, and the latter in several places, for I was very proud. When the trout had been sufficiently admired, we once and for all removed our dumping accident from the credit to the debit side in our account with Fortune.

There was no stopping us now. We fished down to where the Creek enters Lavague, and back up again. When we reached camp we had nine trout. Before we had finished eating those nine, we were unforgettably convinced of the sinfulness of greed. We should have been content when Grandpa had been caught. I ate practically nothing for my lunch but fish. Tom had cannily announced very early in our camping career a restriction on his diet. He professed that he could not eat anything without the accompaniment of bread. At times I wish I had thought of that first. On this occasion, too, he made the quickly rejected proposal that each one of us eat his own catch. The tea was bad.

Our lunch eaten, though not enjoyed, we set forth again. Here is the course, according to the log of a subsequent trip, from the end of the Rock Camp trail to Lavieille Dam.

"Paddle two hundred yards. Lift on right. Paddle one hundred yards. Carry three hundred yards, left; rough. Paddle one hundred yards. Carry five minutes, left; rough. Paddle one hundred yards. Half an hour, more or less, of towing, wading, and paddling; bad stuff. Paddle out into Lake Mallic, left; watch out for old camp past marsh, and land there. Half hour carry to Lavieille Dam."

On our excellent map all that toil and misery, as far as Lake Mallic, is indicated by a neat, almost straight line to mark the course of the Creek, with one small p to suggest one insignificant portage.

Accordingly, we paddled two hundred yards, creeping once more under trees to avoid the current; then we had to unload, carry and re-load, all to cover about twenty yards of distance. We paddled a hundred yards; then made the little carry humorously called rough, in accordance with the playful English device of understatement, used long before King Alfred. We paddled another hundred yards; carried five minutes; paddled a hundred yards; and then came into the most exasperating section of all.

No portaging is provided for in this part. The reason

probably is that most of the travelling on the Creek is done much earlier in the season, when the water is still high. The most recent camp appeared to be at least a month or six weeks old. One hundred yards brought us to a bit of swift water, and we looked carefully about for a portage sign. Undoubtedly there was none: undoubtedly, too, we could not carry through that tangle without a prepared portage. We must paddle up. There was not any great length of bad water here, not more than fifty or sixty yards, and at the top a graceful little white birch beckoned encouragement. We did half the distance without too much trouble; then the canoe suddenly stood still. We were paddling frantically. Tom was lengthening his strokes. I yelled to him to shorten and speed up his stroke. A jagged rock lay ready to receive us if we should swerve aside. Tom shortened with a vengeance, until his arms were working like pistons, but with his paddle barely touching the water before it was jerked out again. We lost a few feet, until he brought his stroke under control and we moved forward almost perceptibly. We stood still again. The birch ahead seemed to be, though it was not, receding, as we strained and fought. I would gladly have gone back and cut a portage, but with us, as with poor old Macbeth, "returning were as tedious as go o'er." Then to our amazement the birch was bending directly over us. We were up. Twice we repeated this same experience, though not again so doubtfully.

In many places the water was very shallow, so shallow that we must wade beside the canoe and pull and lift it along, pleasantly enough wherever the bottom was sandy. In places the current ran swift and deep, among rocks that were barely above or just beneath the surface, with spaces between too short for navigation. In such cases, we worked our way from one rock to another, one of us holding the canoe until the other reached the next rock forward. A rope tied to a paddle would be passed gingerly ahead, and thus the canoe would be handed from one to the other along a dark swirl of brown and green. Sometimes one of us would remain aboard while the other pulled the rope. Tom was lighter and drew less water than I; hence, he was always the passenger, to his great disquiet. We clung with our fingers to cracks in juts of slippery crag. We jammed the canoe between rocks and laboured to release it. We tried prospective channels and had to back down. We hauled ourselves along by means of overhanging spikes of trees, which sometimes broke. We fell into the water. We cut our feet and scratched our hands. At long last we rounded a tough turn and saw before us the blessed opening into Lake Mallic.

At our right was a pleasant little point, and we decided to land for a bit of a smoke and some chocolate. We felt we had earned some indulgence.

"Well, I'll be damned!" cried Tom.

He had discovered a yellow portage sign nailed to a stubby pine on the point. Somewhere we had missed a sign and had thereby given ourselves a series of quite unappreciated experiences. We had no means of knowing how many of these we might have avoided, but we naturally imagined that the portage would have taken care of all the bad stuff. As a matter of fact, we should have been spared about a quarter of a mile.

The doctrine of compensation should not be derided. There is very little doubt in my mind that we should not have been one half so thankful for our little haven as we were, if it had been merely the end of another portage. In such a case, our attention would have been given to Lake

Mallic, and our appreciation of the point would have been restricted to a mild gratitude for a pleasant and convenient push-off for the canoe. Coming after all the turmoil of the previous half-hour, it took on an entirely different character. It was peace.

We lolled in the bracken, beside a growth of ground hemlock, on a south-west slope which provided a grateful bath of sunlight. We lay on our backs under a pine, and soaked in the warmth, for we were wet and chilly from floundering in the Creek and from the anxieties of a dozen precarious moments. Even under the pine, we were not out of the sunlight. We kicked off our shoes. We contracted the universe until space ended where the distinctive character of the point was surrendered to the water and the bush. Like Joshua, we bade time stand still, and it obeyed, in that the past was blotted out, the future had no being, and the present seemed infinite. The perpetual perishings of process were in abeyance; God seemed to be holding his breath. Tom announced that this was a sylvan spot at last, and declared himself ready to camp here for a week. He was very tired of the Creek. Even as he spoke— and this was after twenty minutes, half an hour, an hour, perhaps only five minutes of silence—awareness of the immense systole and diastole of being reawakened in me, and I grew sensitive again to the vast pendulum of time. In other words, I remembered that we had better jog along, with no more cosmic nonsense.

We paddled out into a lake somewhat larger than Lavague, with a much higher shore and an unbroken background of thick woods. I had been over this particular bit only once before, and our directions were not at all explicit. Two silent loons—our first for the trip—floated side by side, and dived at intervals. Had we but known it,

THE ROCK CAMP

they furnished the clue we failed to find, for they were just off the shore from the old camp mentioned in the log, the camp at which we should have landed to begin the mile portage to Lavieille Dam. We could not see the yellow sign, though we paddled slowly round two-thirds of the circumference of the lake. I dimly remembered a portage somewhere in here, but we decided it must be farther up the Creek. A fringe of second-growth hid the old camp, especially from searchers who were on the lookout for fresh portage signs, not grey ruins. I am not sure that the broken-down camp would at that time have suggested the trail, if we had seen it. We later named it the Ghost Camp, not because it was elusive, not because it was more spectral than many other rotting log camps, but because I used there with very peculiar results one of my favourite methods of destroying valuable camera records—I exposed No. 7 without having turned from exposure No. 6.

Having missed the trail, we began once more the weary climb up the Creek, with a repetition, though in mitigated form, of the experiences below Lake Mallic. Each portage sign stirred new hope within us that it was the last: each portage led within a few hundred yards unfailingly back to the Creek. The afternoon was wearing on. After a while, when I realized that we had certainly missed our way, I began to wonder if we should make Lavieille Dam by dark. Theoretically, we could camp anywhere in the bush. All we needed was room to pitch a seven-by-seven tent, which seems to mean only forty-nine square feet, but it is amazing how difficult the finding of those forty-nine square feet may be. As I scanned the shores, with camping-sites in mind, I became oppressed by the inhospitable character of the wild and rocky tangle that borders the Creek between Lake Mallic and Lavieille Dam.

However, the more difficult the country, the more urgent the need that we should camp before nightfall. There are friends of mine who pride themselves on making camp in a strange land by the sense of touch on a pitch-black night. To me, that necessity is calamitous. I was pondering bitterly upon these things as we paddled along one of the occasional stretches of reasonably quiet water, when the counter-irritant of shoaling depth diverted the current of my bitterness.

"We're scraping," said Tom.

"Well, don't I know it?" I replied, crossly. "Push back."

We pushed back, and were afloat again. At that, we were no better off, for the shallowness extended the whole width of the Creek. After we had rammed the canoe viciously into the sand in an exasperated attempt to disprove a plain, inescapable fact, we got out into the water. An hour before, this would not have troubled us, since the footing was quite good, but by now weariness and hope deferred had destroyed whatever amiability we possessed, and we were in a mood when very slight annoyances irritated us. There was sufficient depth to carry Tom, but I made no attempt to prevent his getting out of the canoe.

"Why can't he get out just as well as I can?" I thought. It was ungenerous, for Tom was not one for shirking his share, as I knew quite well.

The water deepened slightly, enough to make the wading more tiring, but not to permit paddling. Forty or fifty yards of this, and the bottom took on an irregularly pebbly character, with an occasional larger stone to snare the unwary foot. I was too discouraged to look ahead, and was startled when Tom stopped with a jerk that nearly threw me off my feet.

"What kind of a rapids is that?" he asked.

I looked up the stream. At first I noted only that the flow of water ceased almost entirely a short distance farther up, and that the bared stones were treacherously piled on one another. Then I saw and understood.

"Tom!" I yelled, "there's your beaver dam!"

I was excited and surprised. I was excited for Tom's sake. From the day when he had found what he called his beaver log, that chunk of wood which he had since been carrying so valiantly, and which he had nearly lost in the dumping episode, I had hoped that we might see a beaver dam. But I certainly had not expected to discover one above the Forks. Nevertheless, here it was, and I was proud of it as one of my Park exhibits.

"Oh, so that's a beaver dam," said Tom, very coolly.

I could see at once that the beaver dam had made a mistake in appearing at this moment. I could see also that Tom was in some subtle, unreasoning way connecting me with the presence of the dam, and assigning the major share of blame for it to me. I forgot that a moment before I had been prepared, in the same unreasoning fashion, to accept credit for it. However, he said nothing further. In a couple of minutes more we had too little water to float the loaded canoe, and were forced to unload it. Tom scarcely glanced at the dam as we carried the stuff up and deposited it beside the quiet pond above. But after we had lifted the canoe across that misery of boulders, I slipped back for a look, and Tom came, too.

There was nothing remarkable about the dam. To confess the truth, the only aspect of a beaver dam that I find remarkable is the fact that beavers have built it, and I am more impressed by the fact when I am out of sight of the dam than when I am standing on it. I think I know the reason. The building of houses and dams by beavers was a source of peculiarly radiant and enduring wonder to my childhood, and somehow I have not made the normal adult adjustment to actuality in this matter. I half expect to see a beaver dam nicely trimmed, with smooth sides and perhaps a small, well-kept bed of flowers. Accordingly, when I find ends of sticks left inartistically showing all over the place, and little appearance of design in the superficial arrangement of tree branches and mud, I am unconsciously disappointed, even though I am forced to recognize that the thing works.

Tom looked about him, not even deigning to sniff. Tom would not have appreciated a beaver dam that day if it had been provided with hydraulic sluice-gates. Turning abruptly, he hurried back toward the canoe. Before I had time to follow, I saw him returning. He was carrying the beaver log. He came up, passed me, strode a few yards along the top of the dam, stopped, and, swinging the piece of wood round his head, hurled it as far as he could out into the water above the dam.

"There, the hell with you!" he cried. "Take your damned old timber and choke on it."

He was addressing the beavers, not me, but no beaver appeared with a retort. He waited a minute.

"Come on, let's get going," he said, impatiently.

I sighed, and fell in behind him. In spite of my own deficiency in appreciation of the marvellous work of beavers, I had thought that Tom would be more stirred by this than by anything else we were likely to see. As a matter of fact, he has since shown gratifying interest in beavers and all their doings. Last summer, he spent the whole of a good fishing evening watching half a dozen beavers in a pool on Crow River. They were merely swimming about and occasionally slapping the water before they dived. All he could see was their wake and a nose at the surface, as one after another would swim past his station, slap the water loudly, and disappear in a splashing swirl of mock alarm. They were evidently playing. Tom sat there entranced until after dark, when nothing could be seen, and all that could be heard was the infrequent noise of the slap, and the snorting of a deer on the other side of the pool. Then, at his suggestion, we went in and left them.

Above the dam the water was of course high, and we had a fair stretch of easy going. Once we were beyond the artificial raising of the stream level by the beaver dam, however, the interminable succession of petty rapids seemed to be beginning again. We had made our clumsy way past three of these, and were steadily but lifelessly paddling along a placid widening, when Tom stopped his paddle stroke in mid-air, leaned forward slightly, and asked,

"Is that wind?"

"What?"

"Either wind or a mighty bad rapids we're coming to. I don't like it."

It made no difference to Tom that we were travelling upstream, and that rapids would cause us no trouble as long as we were below them. He just didn't like rapids; that was all.

I looked up at the trees. There was very little wind, and with a clear sky there could scarcely be any sudden gust coming. Then I listened. It was unmistakable—that low, steady murmur which rises to a distant roar and changes in overtones even while one listens, all without any actual change in the volume of sound. For a few seconds I too yielded to the invisible threat, and half surrendered to a panic fear, as though the thing were coming closer, were coming to overwhelm us. Then I remembered.

"Come on!" I shouted. "That'll be Lavieille Dam."

We paddled up a tiny swift, turned a bend, and saw it, not far ahead. The portage sign was distant enough from the dam to satisfy Tom, though even at that we were drawn quite strongly towards the centre of the wide, slowly revolving, foam-flecked eddy, with its circling booty of leaves and sticks. We were all alive and eager and exuberant. Quickly we beached the canoe, picked up our first loads, and started up the trail to the camp-site, little more than a hundred yards away. Skirting a large rock, with a ravine, perhaps an earlier channel of the Creek, on the other side of the trail, we strode through the tall grass beside the approach to the dam proper, up past the end of this to where the trail from the Ghost Camp, the long trail we had missed on Lake Mallic, comes wandering from the bush. We chose one of half a dozen possible sites, pitched our tent hastily, and made up our beds. Then we feverishly hurried back and brought up everything but the canoe and the fishing tackle. We disposed it all inside the tent. That done, we came out.

It was half-past six. The Dam faces to the east, and as at the Rock Camp, the night shadows come early. The best fishing of the day was to be had in the next twenty minutes. I looked to the west. A cloud was slowly rising from the western horizon, and it seemed to me that if we did not fish immediately, all the sweetness of life would be as apples of Sodom. I know of two trout holes at Lavieille Dam. One is at the right of the dam, within an area twenty or thirty feet square, bounded on the west by the wall of the dam, on the north by the spout of water pouring through the raised gate, on the east by a large, firmly wedged deadhead, and on the south by the high rocky bank of the Creek.

THE ROCK CAMP

About forty yards farther down, where the high rock ends, and the shore drops to near the water level, not far from the place at which the eddy begins, there is the second spot, much better for casting, but not so good for catching.

I was faced with a problem. I knew exactly where to stand, to be quite sure of a rise. I knew also that only one could stand in that one place and fish. There was a second station, but it was not for this first try. I wanted to fish in that good place. It would be no trouble at all to send Tom down to where the good casting was, with a reasonable prospect of trout. On the other hand, I had had up to now somewhat better luck than Tom, since I had caught rather more than he, and had captured the big one. Contentment on his part was essential to a happy trip, even for me. Besides, it would appear a generous gesture for evermore, and would move Tom to feelings of gratitude that might later prove useful. Maybe he would not be able to get any, and I could then have both the credit and the fishing. Finally, I did after all want him to have some enjoyment. So I took him to the good place, showed him where to cast, wished him luck, and started down to the other hole, all puffed up with a consciousness of benevolence and altruism and general angelicity.

Before I was half-way down, I heard him yell. Something must have happened. I rushed back. Tom was weaving his rod back and forth over his head, and it was curved in an arc so full that I expected it to break at any moment.

"I've got two on," he shouted. "I don't believe I hit the water before they were both on."

I held the net ready. Not until the fifth attempt could he work the trout in to where I was able to net them. I disengaged the fish and hooks and line from the net. Tom was dancing. Back to the water again; once more the instantaneous strike. This time I let Tom land his own. In ten minutes we stopped. I had taken two; Tom five. Each of us had lost one. There was no single trout as large as my big one, but the average was much larger than we had found before. We were perfectly content, of course, as we made our way back to the camp.

The cloud above the horizon had thinned out and broken up into gold and silver fragments. Even so, it was full dusk before we finished our meal and our dishes. By this time we realized how tired we were, and a short pipe while the fire burned down was all we wanted.

THE CAMP AT LAVIEILLE DAM

CHAPTER VII

THE LOWER end of Lake Lavieille empties into the Creek by means of a narrow bay, half a mile or so long, out of which the Creek flows in a broad sluggish body of water kept artificially wide by the Dam for perhaps a mile and a half or two miles. The Dam is of fairly recent construction, and is intended to raise the level of the Petawawa River, many miles away, at times when the water is low, and logs that have floated already a hundred miles or more down the little bush creeks must be carried along by the Petawawa to the Ottawa River and the mills. At such times, when the currents are growing lackadaisical, and the logs begin to jam too frequently on sand-bars and low islands, the word goes in, the gate at Lavieille Dam is lifted, and the waters from Lake Lavieille and Dickson Lake go thundering down the Creek.

As you paddle on Lake Lavieille, you will see once in a while a bit of drift moving slowly through the water. It may be a bare pole; or a whole tree, dead these twenty years; or a maimed stump; it may be a straight young pine, the leaves still green, floating because the headland to which it clung so gallantly has been at last eaten too far back by the ceaselessly hungry water. Whatever it is, it is in motion towards the catch-all, the half-moon above the Dam, where it will increase the piled-up mass of derelicts already waiting. Because of this driftwood, the canoe cannot be put into the water immediately above the Dam, but must be carried a few hundred yards farther. We always think of this last bit of trail as having an independent identity, a very charming identity. Although the camp-site, open and grassy because it had been occupied by the builders of the Dam, offered half a dozen locations for the tent, we selected, for some reason obscure at this distance of time, a spot on the very edge of the clearing, just where the little trail sets off for Lake Lavieille.

As I said, we were tired, and when the fire burned down we went to bed, and almost immediately we were asleep.

I woke with a start. There had been some sort of noise near at hand. The tent was all bright. Although I knew it must be near morning, I realized even before I became fully awake that the brightness was from moonlight, not daylight. Again I heard the noise, a scratching sound that seemed to come from inside the tent itself. I raised my head to listen better. Then I saw that Tom, too, was listening. Even as I looked at him, he pointed past me to the corner near my feet. There was nothing, but as I turned away I heard the scratching once more, looked back, and saw, sharply silhouetted against the tent, the perfect outlines of two feet, with the toes widely spread. Something was trying to get into our tent. It reached up as far as it could and pawed at the canvas. Then it withdrew, to reappear at a place a foot or two farther along.

THE CAMP AT LAVIEILLE DAM

While we watched it, without moving except to follow it with our eyes, the creature worked its way in this manner completely round the four sides. Finally, it appeared to be on the point of pushing in under the tent, but though we remained quite still, it suddenly gave up the attempt. I think we both spoke at once. There was a quick scurry, and it was gone.

An insignificant happening, but so utterly delightful that we remained awake to talk about it. Each time since then that we have camped at Lavieille Dam I have dropped off to sleep with the drowsy wish that I might wake up to hear once again that exploratory scratching and to see the two little hands, black and sharply outlined, spread out in the early dawning not twelve inches from my upturned face. For me, when the horns of Elfland blow, as they blew that day, it is usually in the very early morning. Midnight has its witchery, but must have a shiver of apprehension to yield that witchery. Moonlight outdoors has its glamour, but there will be restless desire as an alloy in its golden beauty. Dusk, especially in the country or in the woods or on the water, has its healing. *At even when the sun was set, the sick, O Lord, around Thee lay.* But the beauty of the dusk is quiescent, meditative. Except for milkmen and other conscripts, the very early day, however, has a glory which has been recognized since the morning stars first sang together. There is about it a spaciousness, an expectancy, an adventurous quality that no other time possesses. The hunt is up! Somewhere in it, too, is latent that elfin quality which requires only the most elementary incantation—a bit of grotesquerie, like a rabbit's foot on a tent wall—to set the magic leaping.

We had soaked the prunes overnight, and we put them on to cook, as soon as the porridge was made and the porridge billy free. It required only a very short time to cook them, and we set them on the broken-down remains of an old lumbermen's table to cool, with the billy cover removed. For some reason, we felt lazy that morning, and did not go out for early fishing. We were sitting on the log which served us for bench.

Tom noticed it first, of course, He has an unerring eye for wild life. It was Tom who first saw the five little ones next day, while I saw only two of them, and those only for a second. I was insanely envious, for if there is anything more fascinating than five young chipmunks, the dead spit and image of their parents, I have yet to see it. This was one of the parents of the five. It was sitting on the far end of our log, eating a small piece of bread. That finished, it ran over to the table, up one of the rickety legs, and began eagerly sniffing at the dishes. Finally, it came to the billy in which our prunes had been cooked. They were cool now. The chipmunk climbed up to the rim, and stuck its head inside so far that we were afraid it would fall in. In half a minute it emerged, carrying in its mouth an enormous prune. The delay had evidently been due to its determination to secure the largest possible booty. That chipmunk had been carefully brought up, however; it was conscious of wrong-doing. In its anxiety to get away it stumbled, and dropped its loot, but it quickly seized the prune again and went on its sinful way. It had a good deal of trouble dragging that prune off, and the necessity of avoiding us compelled a tedious detour, but at last it disappeared in the shrubbery. We waited fully fifteen minutes, in the hope of seeing the depredator again; then carefully replacing the cover of the billy, we went down to fish.

A minor distress of the previous evening I did not mention, the discovery that we had left our laundry-and-dish-it hastily retracing the route it had followed, with the birds still attacking. At length we lost sight of the mink, and the birds flew away. This little drama, too, we saw repeated more than once, with apparently the same actors.

A lazy afternoon. There were no black flies, and even the mosquitoes seemed in some mysterious fashion to have gone on holiday. We played an indolent game of cribbage. Still, there was no listlessness in the air. The quiet was the quiet of intense life in equilibrium. There was nothing enervating about it. In other words, this was an afternoon for sharpening the knife, and perhaps the axe. At any rate the knife.

Sharpening your knife in the bush is akin but superior to whittling. It lends itself to meditation; it compels meditation. The technique is so ritualistic that, like the Chinese convention of daily living, it frees the mind to commune within itself or with the Universe. Your little whetstone is brought out. If you are effete, as I am, you fill a cup with water; if you are an ancient he-man, with inexhaustible and sempiternal juices at command, you spit. I suspect that my stone requires no moisture at all, but I was reared on the primitive, thirsty grindstone, and I cannot become a dry in mid-life. You sit down on a log, or better still, a stump, and fill your pipe. You squint along the edge to see where the knife is dullest, and begin. From then on, the operation is automatic. Even your preoccupation with the problem of whether separate personal identity is real or an illusion need scarcely be disturbed by the appraising glance, or the tentative feathery movement of your thumb across the edge. As a blessed heritage from the days when your remote ancestor took a month off to work out the nick in his best stone axe, the sharpening of your knife is done by agencies hidden deep in the recesses of being, agencies long dormant, but which call into activity with them the contemplative powers of the soul.

From all this you will gather that I had a good time at this job. If you have ever sharpened your hunting knife, you will understand. If, moreover, you are shy and decently modest, you will maintain that I am talking nonsense, that when sharpening his knife a man does not need to do any thinking at all, and therefore does none. If, however, you are less ashamed of thought, you will recall the dropping away of querulousness and worry, the rich sense of harmony, which indicate the listening spirit.

I suppose that sharpening a scythe would be the same. But it must be with a hand stone. There is no meditation in the grindstone, for with it the age of machinery has begun. The man who invented the wheel must have thought profoundly; not so the man who turns it. The grindstone is at one end of the assembly line. I know, for I have turned the grindstone; also I have held the axe against it. Holding the axe demands close attention, and is a skill. Turning the grindstone is a degrading thing, producing bitter thoughts, if any. It is a form of treadmill.

At four o'clock we were down at the Dam. Tom was below, out on a bit of rock, casting. I was leaning against the timbers of the Dam itself, having found this a pleasant, cool spot on a hot day. Fifteen feet away, the water poured through, a spout of white power, perhaps three and a half feet thick and about twelve feet wide, with a lather of foam extending twenty or twenty-five feet beyond the spout. An ethereal rainbow spanned the length of this foam. The under side of the curving spout combined with the timbered face of the Dam and the Creek level to form a green, mysterious segment of a hollow cylinder within which I have always dreamed the fabulous monster trout is lurking. I still waste a good deal of time trying for that fish. There came once a season when the vision of that great trout had become greatly enfeebled. Then suddenly, one day, Tom came running down with a wild story of a bit of bait thrown into the greenish chamber, of a tornado attack that dragged half a hundred yards of line out before he could begin to attempt any control, of a plunging second when he caught up the slack, and then of a brand-new leader snapped off and lost forever. On this afternoon, however, Tom's encounter with the monster was still two years in the future, faith was languid, and I was idly flicking a line into the water at the outer edge of the spout. Nothing was rising to flies, and we had forsworn worms for the day.

Tom came up to report that a trout had snatched a blue moth floating on the surface. Accordingly, I went down and tried the Silver Doctor. The trout took one supercilious sniff at it. Tom ran down a moth of the same variety as the one he had seen picked off, and tried it, without success, although three or four that dropped on the water of their own accord were instantaneously seized. Since the blue of the moths almost exactly matched the blue of my Silver Doctor, I could not understand the lack of interest until it occurred to me to examine one of the moths. Tom obligingly caught another for me. Though blue above, it proved to be white beneath, and therefore presumably white to the fish. I took off the Silver Doctor and tried a whitish fly, with perfect but utterly misplaced confidence. After that, Tom chased down a dragon-fly, and wasted its innocent life.

Now I know quite well what a fisherman does in such circumstances. He catches the blue moth, examines it carefully, and then from his little kit he takes out the proper materials and, having constructed a perfect copy of the moth, he invents and names a new fly. He thereupon reels in trout to the point of utter boredom.

I put on a worm and got the trout. By that time it was a quarter to six; time to light the fire for another meal, if we wished to have any evening fishing. As I think I have said, night falls early upon the fishing holes at the Dam. We were not very anxious to eat fish, but we were eager to catch them, even if it necessitated eating them.

Trout came easily that evening—much too easily. After less than half an hour of fishing, Tom wanted to stop. He refused to face the breakfast prospect past the ninth. But the ninth was the best of all, and Tom had caught it. The eighth, which was mine, had been next in size. Now no man should be asked to retire with a rising tide of fortune like to that: no fisherman will be asked by a fellow-fisherman to do so. I caught the tenth, fully an inch and a half longer than the ninth. When the eleventh and the twelfth kept up the mocking progression, we recognized the hideous dilemma. Neither one of us had the slightest doubt that we could go on catching trout all night—trout that would be huger and huger, until about half an hour after dark we should engage in a terrific duel with a Trout to which Nipigon's proudest would be but as a minnow. Nor had we any doubt of our ability to land that final mesozoic creature. For we saw the horrible joke. We should land that trout because we'd be obliged to eat it. Imagination staggered about drunkenly; then reason resumed what little sway she normally has over us. Heart-broken, we quit, and watched opportunity go galloping off with sardonic mirth, its single lock, once grasped, released again.

We cleaned those trout above the Dam, and at the same time watched the last changing sunset colours. We returned to camp, coaxed the fire back into a gentle activity, and sat silent on our log. Dusk crept over the camp and the woods grew quiet, except for the low grumble of the Dam. A family of rabbits came out, played hide-and-seek among our feet, and fell to feeding on the lush clover, sown without the will of man though not without the agency of horses in the busy years when the Dam had been a-building. We kept still, and even let our pipes go out. After a time a mosquito caught me exactly between the shoulder-blades and I could not help slapping at it. The rabbits scampered away, and did not return while we were up.

The time was propitious for review, for reminiscence. Tom poked the fire until it burned up brightly. We recalled to each other all the incidents, many of them now long since forgotten, that had made the trip seem crowded with adventures; mostly unassociated with that nettle Danger; almost all, indeed, belonging to the category of adventure only for children, of normal size or overgrown.

A remark in connection with our dumping episode gave me a new and startling insight into the miraculously possible. We had been reminding ourselves of the brief glimpse we had had of a most unalluring prospect, the prospect of going down the half-mile or more of wildly plunging water whose real ferocity begins some thirty yards below the place we had selected for upsetting the canoe.

"I wouldn't go down that rapids," said Tom. "I'd get out."

I looked up at him. He had thrown on the fire a couple of branches of balsam, remains of what had been a balsam bed, and once more it blazed in momentary splendour. I looked to see if he were joking, but the expression of his face was in keeping with the quiet, earnest confidence of his tone.

"Get out?" I said. "How?"

"I'd fly."

Just that. He believed he could have flown, if necessary, out of that extremity, and I am bound to confess that I believed it too. The removal of mountains by faith was a familiar and accepted idea, but never before that moment had I realized the dynamic of desperation. Absorbed in the contemplation of this new vista of experience, I allowed the conversation to languish. We sat there in silence until the fire burned down to embers; then we picked our way through the wet grass to the tent.

Tom won the rubber of cribbage, leaving the count 6-3 on the series for the trip. I put the pegs away. We had been making up our collective mind, and as usual, the decision had been reached before the subject was broached.

"It's a great camp," said Tom. "Especially with all these little animals around."

I agreed.

"Pity the fishing's getting so good."

"Yes. Six apiece for breakfast. Time you put six trout on top of your porridge you'll have enough for a light breakfast."

"Suppose we'll have to be getting along some of these days. We've had a good rest."

"I guess so. How about tomorrow, if it's a good day?"

"Okay."

The sentimental soul is very feline, and clings tenaciously to places. It can sit down under a gourd and call it home. It can attach itself to a protean cloud, and grieve when the cloud breaks up. It can find itself a rotting stump beside a raw camp-site, and look upon that stump as the threshold of its ancient family seat. Near the so-called Glory Hole, Tom and I camped three successive years. The fourth year we found a group of men with red shirts and broad-axes, putting up a ranger's cabin. We had intended to camp there, but with bitterness and hatred in our hearts we paddled on another two miles to the Island of the Pines. We regarded those innocent woodsmen with the same loathing with which I fancy a sensitive FitzLacy regards the American button manufacturer who has just bought the castle given to the first FitzLacy by an early Plantagenet in return for a useful murder.

Accordingly, we experienced the pangs of homesickness as we thought of breaking up our camp next day. It is a mistake to remain more than one night in one place, we agreed. Our neighbours were irreplaceable. Our chipmunk would break its heart. Our rabbits would cavort about in vain. Is it not axiomatic that the universe is meaningless without man? The rose born to blush unseen does not blush at all. Of course not. It may have chemical processes, but it cannot blush. Thoughts like these, on the emptiness of the camp-site when we should be gone, afflicted us, but not for long, for we were sleepy.

THE CAMP ON LAKE LAVIEILLE

CHAPTER VIII

THE NEXT morning there seemed no need for hurry. To be sure, we had, like Nuvoletta, made up our myriad of drifting minds to move that day, but the day was most comfortably mapped out. We should be paddling only half an hour or so. At the outer end of the narrow bay that leads the waters of Lake Lavieille into the Creek there is a point. I had never set foot on it, but it was enticing, had a camp-site ready, and seemed the easiest introduction of Tom to lake canoeing. If we reached this spot in the afternoon, in time to camp, sup, and be out for a bit of evening trolling, it would be soon enough.

Accordingly, we lolled about that morning. We ate our fish, but Tom refused his porridge. We fed the chipmunk. We even fished in a half-hearted manner, catching five unwanted trout of goodly size. At half-past ten we went to take down the tent.

Although we have our conventions, we have no pride, no sense of decency. I am sure that respectable tent-dwellers drive in neat little rows of pegs and stakes, if the terrain permits it at all—stakes for the tent-ropes and pegs for the little loops at the bottom of the tent wall. I am convinced that campers worthy of the franchise and a permit use a proper ridge pole, and do whatever is meet in setting up their tent.

We do none of these things. We dislike tent-stakes, using them only in the last extremity, unless a previous party has left a good set lying exactly where we wish to pitch our tent. Otherwise we have two methods, according to circumstances. If they are available, we roll boulders somewhere near the tent-site, and wrap our tent-ropes round them. Then we push these boulders about until we have removed the most outrageous of the creases in the tent. If it is only for one night, does not look like rain, and is quiet, we frequently leave the tent in a deplorably untidy condition, askew and wrinkled, sagging in the centre and with one side higher than the other. Only by accident would our tent convey any impression of neatness. If boulders are not available, we usually hunt up a couple of fallen trees, cut off two twelve-foot lengths, and lay one of these along each side. Sometimes we thread the log through our rope loops, but more often we tie the ropes around the log and disregard the loops entirely. If possible, we wedge the ends of the log behind a tree, or place on each end some heavy weight. Any pair of boys who would venture to set up a tent in any boys' camp in as sloppy a manner as we do would be considered a baneful influence and sent home at once. And quite properly.

We cut five poles if we must; that is, if we do not find some discarded ones. We have a rope running along the ridge of the tent, on the inside, knotted so that it will not slip through the canvas. This rope extends about twenty feet beyond each end. We try to find a spot between two trees, in order that our ridge rope may be secured to solid supports. We will sacrifice a good deal of bottom comfort for this indolent solution of the tent-staying problem. Failing trees, a stump will serve us, or a log, or a heavy stone. We do have qualms at times, if that will help our case with the jury. At the Dam we used rocks. We stayed the tent with boulders; we pegged it with boulders and heavy fragments from blasting operations.

At half-past ten, as I said, we went to take down the tent. As a precautionary formality, I glanced at the sky. Over in the west a cloud the bigness of a man's hand was groping over the horizon into an otherwise clear sky. At the beginning of the trip, such a presage would have sent us scurrying to get away into the next camp, but two days of idling had made us lazy. We seized the excuse for inaction and went back down to the Dam to fish listlessly in the blazing sunlight. We caught six more in about twenty minutes and retreated in terror. We had eaten twelve good trout for breakfast; we now had eleven for lunch. I may say that in order to gain credence, I have understated the number of trout we actually caught—and ate—on that night and morning.

Imagination works less effectively in broad day, beneath the white light that beats upon a shadeless dam in midsummer, than among the furtive nuances of the forest twilight. Experience, if only three or four hours old, speaks with authority. We both knew that we could eat no more than we had now taken: Tom knew that he could not gorge his share even of those.

At that, it was a most uncomfortable meal. I ate nothing but fish, because I was not in the least hungry for anything. Tom ate his share of the bread and mine too, protesting as usual that he could not eat a mouthful of fish without a corresponding amount of bread.

At half-past twelve, the dishes washed, we took the canoe down to the water. The small cloud was expanding, but slowly. We were standing beside the yellow portage sign, looking at the sky and bush and water.

"Hell!" said Tom, with a groan. "It's all spoiled."

"What's the matter? What's spoiled?" I asked, startled.

"Isn't that a canoe out there?"

I looked out in consternation, with the hope that whatever he had seen might prove to be a floating log, but with only a faint hope, because I knew Tom's keenness of sight. By the time I found it, there was no doubt. A red canoe, with two men, was moving steadily towards us.

Perhaps the exaggerated craving for privacy engendered in the woods has something to do with it. Perhaps the shattered illusion of remoteness. Perhaps the outraged sense of propriety, of vested interest, of ancient privilege. No sense of proprietorship can be stronger that that which inheres in a camp-site occupied an hour ago, in a fishing hole possessed ten minutes. At any rate, we look upon all newcomers as trespassers, poachers, thieves and pirates. We think of them as flabby, plague-ridden, scrofulous, dollar-dirty city slickers, come to prey upon and contaminate us, the noble savages. We imagine they are probably gangsters, fleeing from the law, and armed with sub-machine-guns and sawed-off shotguns. We stare at them with a malignancy that is anything but cold.

This was the Welcome mat that our hospitable spirits spread before the strangers. They approached to within some three hundred yards of us, then they stopped and looked at us. They appeared to be fussing with something in the canoe. We could hear, though we could not distinguish their voices. They must have waited thus three or four minutes before they resumed their paddling and pushing among the stumps and logs and ends of floating trees which sometimes almost block this landing-place, and came to rest beside us.

"Hello," said Tom.

"Hello."

They were young lads, of high-school age, with a very resplendent outfit, as far as the appointments of their canoe and dunnage were concerned. A beautiful chestnut canoe, with a frame for the axe, rings for the paddle lashings, and the spare paddle fitted to the side; new bags; knives like gleaming cutlasses in their belts; ready-made tent-poles—all these, and more that I have forgotten. Their own clothes were in tatters, and undoubtedly had been close to tatters when they left home.

As soon as we noticed this perfect appreciation of the relative importance given to camping and personal outfits, our hearts warmed to them at once. They were too new for experience to have taught them; it could only have been instinct: and anyone to whom instinct had revealed the proper values in these matters was of the tribe. Still more did their reticence enchant us. After this first greeting they went about their business without a further word to us, though not without a covert glance or two. Without a word they started up the trail.

Then we had a rear view of them, and Tom whistled under his breath. The younger, slighter of the two had nothing whatever between him and anything he wished to sit upon. I looked at Tom, and we both shuddered. In the quiet we could hear the roar of millions of mosquitoes being born into a hungry world. Then we walked slowly after them towards camp.

Our two visitors were there. As we approached, they lowered the canoe from their shoulders. The older came over to us.

"Could you tell us which of these trails leads to the Petawawa?" he asked.

We told him, and impelled by the spectacle of dire necessity we had just seen, asked him if they had a good supply of fly-dope. They had, but the offer pleased them, and they were very appreciative of the two chocolate bars we gave them. I wanted to offer them a piece of mending canvas and a needle and thread, but I could not be sure of whether they were ashamed or proud of their plight.

We asked them how the fishing had been. They didn't know, for they were making a fast, light trip, with barely grub to last to Brent, and no time for fishing, unless a speedy lake trout could seize their troll lure as it hurtled past.

"Gee! I'd like some speckled trout," said the younger one, as they resumed their load and set off, with smiles and parting greetings.

"He wishes he had some speckled trout!" Tom muttered. "He wishes he had some speckled trout. If he had only come an hour ago."

A grin spread over his face.

"Do you know why those boys didn't want to come in?"

"Why?"

"They were scared of us."

I knew it, and I have rarely been so flattered in my life. I immediately hunted out a mirror from my little haversack. Then I lent it to Tom.

There was nothing to keep us longer at the Dam. No matter how quickly the two boys had been swallowed up again by the woods, no matter how fully they had established their right to be in the woods, they had crashed our solitude and the camp was done. We packed our stuff, leaving the ground-sheets out, in case of rain, and started. Tom thought he saw the chipmunk running across the trail behind us, but he could not be sure.

We loaded the canoe and nosed our way out through the debris, pushing it aside when we could, making our way round it when we could not move it. A hundred yards more, and the murmur of the Dam began to die down, to leave for a time a queer uneasiness. The Creek widened, the deadheads began to thin out. On our left, the dreary stretch of drowned land, with its gaunt, lifeless trees, told of the growth sacrificed to pile Lake Lavieille against the Dam. On our right there was not the same desolation, for the high bank had protected the forest. We paddled past the tablet-shaped rock that tells us, as we come the other way, that we have little more than fifteen minutes to go before we reach the portage. We slid round a point—too close to suit Tom, who could see rocks—and were in the bay. Over on the far side of this bay was the headland for which we were steering. I picked out a tall pine and tried to keep it bobbing up and down directly over Tom's left ear.

The canoe began to roll with the freshening breeze, and the sky darkened, as we headed more or less diagonally across the bay. I was somewhat nervous, not over the threat of rain, but because of the wind. I had forgotten how completely we had been able to disregard the wind in the quiet, sheltered depths of the inland forest. Henceforth, the wind was to be the deciding factor in our movements. I was uncertain as to how Tom would be in open-water paddling, with a breeze blowing and white water showing ahead, but I need have had no fears for him. In dubious weather on a lake, he is much happier than I am.

We reached the headland, pulled the canoe ashore and hurried to get the tent up. A few drops of rain were falling, and the waters of the lake beyond the point were torn and white. The wind died down. The rainstorm burst as we were putting the last of our bundles into the tent, and we sat inside and glowed with the intense satisfaction that follows the close call, the peril past. We had made camp; we had kept our stuff dry; we had that very desirable comfort, a dry tent-bottom.

There was a succession of squalls, but in an hour, at most, the rain ceased, the sun came out, and we ventured forth to view our grounds. They were worth the viewing, and to us, accustomed to the restricted world of a camp buried in the woods, they were especially delightful. From some words scrawled on a weather-beaten signboard tacked upon a tree, we derived the name Hayes Point. That may or may not be its official name, if it has any, but it is Hayes Point to us. It is forty or fifty feet above the lake level, and it is covered with pines, of no great size, but pines. Accordingly, there is no undergrowth. The fireplace and table are well back from the tip of the point, so that the tent may be given some shelter from the wind and still be close to cooking operations.

Lake Lavieille is one of the three larger lakes with which this narrative has to do. The others are Opeongo and Dickson. All three have sharply differentiated characters, if not personalities. A dear friend who knows Opeongo almost as well as he knows the Upanishads is convinced that Opeongo is animated by a sinister Spirit which broods unsleepingly, malevolently, over the three great arms of that majestic water. Another friend, whose belief in any kind of spirits is limited to those over a certain per cent proof, also regards Opeongo as intimidating, but he believes it intimidating only because he considers it dangerous to venturesome canoeists, with its great open bays. Whether he finds it dangerous because of the unrecognized presence of the malevolent deva, or whether my first friend finds the local malevolent deva because of an unrecognized perception of the lake's dangerous character, I will not pretend to determine. Since I had not seen Opeongo before my two friends had told me about it, I have had difficulty in building up my own conception of the personality that dominates it. Anyway, there are cottages and motor-boats on Opeongo, and Tom and I regard it as a suburb of Toronto.

Dickson Lake is lonesome, as well as lonely. It is a strange, remote water, with dark moods and a wildness unknown to our other lakes. It is not very large, and it is narrow. It bends almost at a right angle. It has one great high island and several smaller ones. It is shallow in many places, and can get up a sea more quickly than any other lake I know. It is the rendezvous of loons.

Lavicille, from Hayes Point, is a lake of faery. Although the main body, to the west and north-west, is hidden behind its one big island, haunt of the great horned owl, a long, eager, unnamed bay, its tip away in the south-west, provides a vista from the Point. To the south, the shore leads us off in the direction of Hardy Bay. Thither we shall be going, when we move next. There are eight or ten islands. Some of them, like the two on the way to Dickson Lake that mark the end of a lee, are set sturdily down, with their roots reaching deep and clutching the foundations of the earth itself. Others, like Tom's island, so called because of a minor landing necessity, rest delicately though immovably on the bosom of the lake—whatever that may be. Others again, some two or three, like the gossamer isle behind which Jim and I sought shelter one breath-taking day, merely poise dainty feet on the shimmering surface. The far horizon, usually misty blue, billows in a range of undulations, and beyond them the huge round masses of the great hills beside Big Crow Lake lift their shadowy bulks. I suppose that Lavieille derives its peculiar glamour from these physical features, but in that enchanted world I can easily suspend my disbelief in lake spirits and divinities. On Lavieille, as nowhere else for me, the long light shakes across the lake.

The storm was over and the sun was out, but the wind had not fallen. It was a cool wind, and it blew across that point in a way to which we inlanders were not accustomed. I went back into the tent for my mackinaw. Tom had put on his leather jacket. We moved energetically, purposefully and briskly going nowhere.

"When do you want to start the fire?" Tom asked, about half-past four.

I felt exactly the same way. I was hungry, and I was chilly. Those five and a half large trout had made a distressingly full lunch, but I began to anticipate the next meal with keen relish. There would be no fish. I wanted something hot, new, substantial. Once again the miracle of communication was wrought. Tom took the idea, so to speak, out of my mouth.

"How are chances for some pancakes?"

Earlier in this narrative I mentioned that I should by preference go into the bush without any bread at all, and depend entirely upon pancakes. (I want to call them flapjacks, owing to a boyhood passion for western stories, but I can't quite bring myself to it. I have known them too long and intimately, and always as pancakes, in real life.

THE CAMP ON LAKE LAVIEILLE

I once disappointed two Connecticut youths by my failure to recognize them under the name of bannocks. "All Canadians in the woods make bannocks, don't they?" they asked me plaintively.) At the beginning of my camping career I carried this breadless idea into practice, but when I first went out with Jim I found myself eating baker's

bread, and eating it with avidity. On this present trip I had learned that Tom counts that meal lost in which he has not broken and eaten bread. The result has been that in our trips pancakes serve, not as a staple, but as a pleasing variation in the menu. As time passes, and the bread grows drier and mouldier, the pancakes become more and more welcome, and finally essential.

A hesitation assails me at this point, if a hesitation can assail. One of the harmless affectations which I assume with Tom must be exposed, and exposed before him. Most of my affectations of woodcraft were put on for Tom with the quite laudable object of reducing his reasonable doubts of my ability to get him safely out of the bush into which I was enticing him. I simply was compelled to affect a proficiency in woodcraft that I was only too conscious of lacking. Otherwise, he would never have come at all.

But my pancake affectation springs from sheer vanity and exhibitionism. All my life I have heard and read of cowboys and miners and other real men who made flapjacks; and all of them tossed the flapjacks with one hand, while with the other they nonchalantly picked off an Injun or roped a maverick. I have made pancakes for many years, but used prosaically to turn them with a common knife. Once, however, in a mood like that of Tartarin before he did finally go lion-hunting, I had been tempted beyond my strength to allow it to be believed that I was a wild man from the North. It was a gorgeous experience until the unanticipated occasion when I was called upon to make good my claims, during one of my first camping trips. At that time, I remember, I had judged it necessary to essay the tossing of flapjacks. I may, indeed, have conveyed the impression, if not the information, that I had tossed pancakes from about the age of seven. By dint of secret and somewhat wasteful practice I had been able to please my not very critical audience at that time. How I managed secret practice on a camping trip I do not remember.

This accomplishment, learned furtively and from fictional memory, I had preserved precariously from year to year, never sufficiently sure of myself in it to be comfortable and genuinely self-possessed. Nevertheless, I basked in the delightful admiration of the very young; and I was to some extent reassured by the lack of interest displayed by any old-timers before whom I might have to do my flipping. Now I had to perform the old trick once more. Tom had a taste in westerns even lower than mine, if possible, and better sustained. Mine had become somewhat antiquarian. I knew that he would be greatly encouraged and lifted up in spirit if I tossed the damned things.

Tom mixed the Klim and I made a batter. Since the pancake flour we use is always ready prepared, even to salt, there is nothing left to do but hit upon a right consistency and cook 'em. My first one is almost invariably too thick, my second far too thin. The result of this order in my trial and error method of cooking is that we are usually compelled to eat more pancakes than we bargain for. The addition of water or Klim to thin the batter does not add materially to the actual pancake content of the camping stomach; the addition of flour to thicken does.

Another disturbing factor must be mentioned. Our frying-pan is of light steel, and very thin. Consequently, through the years, its frying surface has ceased to be the monotonously level plain we purchased, and has taken on the interesting character of low, rolling country. Now grease, like water, seeks the lowest level, and the nicely measured amount of grease necessary for the elegant perfection of my pancakes leaves the steely hills bare. The pancakes stick and burn on these heights. Some time we must buy a new frying-pan.

My first pancake ran true to form and was too thick. Hence it remained nicely in the centre of the pan. The bubbles rose slowly, but they rose. I slid a knife around under it, as unobtrusively as possible, and jiggled the pan about until my pancake moved freely. Then I took the pan off the fire and held it over some fairly clean grass. Tom was watching me with evident interest. With all the grace and abandon of a middle-aged novice taking his first swing with a brassie, I tossed the pancake—perfectly.

L'audace! Toujours l'audace! Coquettish fortune had smiled once more on imposture. Tom was satisfied. It did not matter that half of my next pancake wrapped itself tenderly around the outside of the frying-pan, and had to be destroyed.

There is a most acceptable by-product in pancake making. The frying-pan never blooms so fair as after pancakes. At all other times there lingers about it an air of incomplete cleansing, even when it has been boiled and scoured and soaped and laboured with. But after pancakes it wears a smiling morning face of utter purity. I suppose that we eat in the pancakes whatever of accumulated grubbiness is removed in their frying, but what of that! The cleanliness obtained with hot water and soap is at best a negative sort of virtue, a mere absence of evil; the condition left by pancakes is a glowing positive good, making glad the heart of man. The last pancake—it may be a small, irregular thing that sprawls and hunches up uneasily in the middle, or it may be a huge monopolistic mass that must be turned with deftness—the last pancake fried and eaten, you enjoy the assurance that you have fed on pancakes from a contented pan.

We were ready now for an hour's trolling. Anyone who has ever held a troll at all knows more about it than I do, but in these later years, the trouting years of my life, I pretend to myself and to others that I used to know a good deal about trolling for bass. In the years when I trolled with Jim, and he landed all his strikes, while I usually lost mine, he constantly admonished me to carry out some mysterious operation which was designed to end any pretty trifling with the hook on the part of the fish. He had a technical name for it, but I have forgotten that. I never understood what he was talking about anyway, and my tacit claims to experience prevented my asking him.

In one respect, however, this first troll out from Hayes Point was a vast relief. We were about to use a brand-new copper line, and there was no point in pretending that I knew all about copper lines. Not only had I never used one before, but I had never seen one used. I had had at one time a confused sort of idea that the line was a cable, approximating in size to the mooring cables of fair-sized ships, and that it was reeled in round a sort of capstan, slowly, to the tune of *Haul Away Joe*. I heard of lines three hundred, four hundred, five hundred feet long, and my untutored imagination saw those lines descending like a plummet and capturing strange monsters, known as grey trout, which swam about forever at those vast depths. The very word *grey* conveyed to me a mysterious impression of unearthliness and ruthlessness when applied to trout. Jim did not use a copper line. He normally trolled with a fly or possibly a worm and little spinner of some sort, on a dinky little fly-rod.

One result of his type of trolling was that we had never caught any very large lake trout. We heard, with varying degrees of incredulity, of huge fish being taken all around us, but that was all. In my silent opinion, all that we lacked, in order to get the big ones, was a copper line. I could see myself laying down and measuring a string of giants about which I too could boast, quietly, and as if the catching of such was a routine matter with me. All this I could see, if I only had a copper line. In preparation for this trip, then, I had bought one, the cheapest. The reel struck me as small, but I was assured by my tactful salesman that it was a standard size, and large enough for anything up to tarpon.

When we set out that evening, it was with the new copper line. We laboured under two recognizable disadvantages. The first was ignorance as to the proper depth at which we should be trolling; the second a complete lack of knowledge as to how deep we were trolling. We tried various devices for determining depth, based on rough calculations of the angle made by the line and the water surface, together with an estimate of the line out, reckoned by the diminution on the spool. On shore we had taken the preliminary step of reeling out the line and noting the bulk on the reel at various lengths, but it was not very helpful.

We paddled half an hour without a strike. Then we had two in quick succession. We turned in a wide arc and retraced our course, but without success. We went out into the sunset past the far end of the big island, and let out line recklessly. There were two possible reasons for our failure to catch anything. We were paddling too fast, or we had not enough line out. We remedied both conditions. Nothing happened. Tom suggested a little speeding up, and this produced results immediately. We had both been paddling, and I had the rod and reel tucked under my leg and over a thwart in such a way as I thought would allow the reel to revolve, but would permit me to see and seize the rod before anything decisive could happen. There was a sudden jerk. I stopped paddling, called to Tom to keep on, and grabbed for the rod. The Thing began to pull backward, and I was forced to reel out frantically. In a little while the heavy pull eased off, and I was afraid the fish was gone. I reeled in and called to Tom to paddle hard again. Once more I felt the heavy jerk, and I breathed freely. Tom was paddling slowly, waiting. My fear now was that our prey would decide suddenly to come to the surface. I wanted to keep it down until it was completely exhausted. Then, if necessary, we could land, and beach it in the course of time. We had a good hour yet, and we were perfectly willing to devote it all to this one fish.

I had been in the habit of scoffing at trolling as not fishing at all, and I had especially scorned the notion of sport that would permit a man to hook a fish on an enormous stretch of line, a length so great that the fish, half-drowned before it ever reached the surface, was dragged limply over the gunwale. None of my ideas or remarks on this subject were in the slightest degree reflections of actual experience; they were merely ignorant parrotings of the remarks of other men who may or may not have had any more experience than I. At any rate, my most passionate desire at this time was that I might be able to keep the fish down until it was not only exhausted, but actually dead. I did not wish to run any risk of losing a catch which was in an entirely different category from anything I had ever hooked before. The fish showed no inclination to come to the top. Once or twice there was a momentary slackening of the line which indicated that it might be on its way to the surface, but each time it apparently changed its mind.

I do not know how long this patient duel went on. The sun set in glory, and I was conscious of the fittingness of such a sunset for such a crowning moment in our lives. Tom was paddling slowly round and round, just enough to keep the line taut. The trout—it could be nothing but a lake trout—had changed its position very little. It seemed to be weakening, however, for, though there was still the heavy pull, there was nothing spasmodic. There had really been nothing spasmodic from the beginning. Finally the moment came. I announced that I was about to reel in. Tom had the landing-net ready, a pitifully small receptacle for the present purpose. The creature resisted, sullenly, obstinately, heavily. Suddenly it gave up. The line was coming in with no effort at all, and for an instant I feared the trout might be off. Tom reassured me by his confident and sensible comment, that it must be thoroughly well hooked after all that struggle. I watched the water and the line anxiously.

It could not have been in the water very long, for some bark was still firmly hooked when we pulled in the troll, enough to show that our lake trout had been at one time a flourishing pine.

We had just made camp, had carried the canoe up, and had strolled to the extreme point to watch the last bits of colour in the west, when the loons began. There had been those two silent loons on Lake Mallic, and at Lavieille Dam we had heard a solitary one three or four times, but we had hitherto been inland, too far inland, too distant from lakes, to hear them at their best. We had regretted this, for to both of us the loon's cry is the most characteristic sound of the Ontario bush.

As far as our unscientific observation goes, the loons in the Park have three calls. One of the three Tom likes best; the second he regards as my favourite; the third both of us consider unworthy of loons. This third we have heard most frequently on Dickson Lake. It is an irregular sort of wild and noisy medley, and there is a barbaric, unrestrained quality to it which makes us suspect the baneful influence of white civilization. It is, of course, musical, as any sound made by a loon is bound to be, and I imagine sometimes that it resembles one or two short passages in the first movement of Stravinsky's *Rite of Spring*, but when I hear the loons my memory of the Stravinsky is too dim, and when I hear the Stravinsky my memory of the third cry is far too attenuated.

The second cry has been most frequently maligned as the 'maniacal laughter' of the loon. Nothing I know of is less maniacal. It is regular, purposeful, coherent. It is pre-eminently social. It is, to be sure, a mysterious, a baffling, a cryptic cry. It can do magical tricks with numbers. If the illusion of a multitude of loons were ever desired, only two would be required. I have listened on a lonely lake, and have been convinced that all the loons in the whole area, to the number of twenty at least, were gathered on that laké, only to find upon investigation that but two loons were in the vicinity. There is an aid to this illusion, for nowhere is the echo, Nature's ancient re-broadcasting system, more effective than in the reproduction of the loon's wild calls. Many an evening, too, we have listened to that haunting halloo and its answers, convinced that the birds themselves were over by the far shore, if not on some other lake, and have discovered the pair floating less than a hundred yards away. The sound of the loon is always away off yonder. I suppose that the rapid repetition of the same clear, ringing notes does suggest laughter, but the almost invariable association with it of the qualifying demoniacal or maniacal has prejudiced me against the whole expression. The effect is too thrilling, too poignant, for laughter.

Perhaps *poignant* should be reserved for the third cry, the cry that most entrances Tom. Usually it is the first heard, in our section of the Park. Without any warning, there comes drifting from far away that lonely, sorrowful cry for comfort. I suppose that it, too, comes from some two or three hundred yards away, but we have not known this, and to both of us that single, prolonged wail of desolation remains unlocated, in a distant world of solitude and longing. It is a lonesome cry, filled with infinite yearning, with at times a spectral quality of disembodiment.

Just at dusk, that night, the loons put on their concert. It may have lasted for twenty-five minutes or half an hour. Into it there broke at times from the big island the booming hunting-call of the Great Horned Owl. I trust that the cry comes from the Great Horned Owl. I know that it is from some kind of owl. I have thought of asking some authority about it, but have been deterred by a lingering doubt as to whether the Universe shares my conception of order. It would be faith-shattering to discover that the great call did not belong to the Great Horned Owl. I dare not risk the investigation, for while I protest a boundless regard for truth, I recognize the necessary precedence of comfort over truth. I want it to be the Great Horned Owl. Anyway, aesthetic truth has a higher value than mere fact.

Owls have disappointed us quite often. Tom had two great, unfulfilled desires—to see a bear in the bush, and to hear the howling of wolves, also in the bush. I had the same two desires, but in my case they were not unfulfilled ones. Next to loons, I like best to hear wolves, in the distance. I do not care for the yapping that is associated, I am told, with the kill, and which I have heard often enough to satisfy me, but I do enjoy the long, plaintive howl of the harmless Ontario wolf.

Now above all else Tom wishes to have heard wolves. As a result, his insistent credulousness in this respect is sometimes positively embarrassing. If there is any unwonted cry in the night that cannot be identified, Tom wills it so ardently to be wolves, that the temptation to gratify him is very strong. These indefinite cries have to be credited in most cases to owls. This night we were much too close to leave any room even for Tom to dream of wolves,

ON THE LAKES

CHAPTER IX

Tom was very grave next morning when he opened the bread bag. I have already mentioned his dependence upon bread. He took out a loaf, brought it over to the table, and cut a slice.

"This looks bad," he said, and his reference was primarily to the situation, though very applicable to the bread.

Three days before he had observed the first disquieting symptoms of decay, an irregular green streak along a crease in one of the loaves. Since then, like ivy creeping over the old church tower, it had been spreading and penetrating. Tom was inclined to blame the dipping of the bread in the water at the time of our upsetting, but I doubt if that had done more than cooperate with the inevitable. As far as my experience with it is concerned, ordinary bread kept more than a week or so on a camping trip tends to mould. The only variation is in the speed of the process.

I do not really know that green bread mould is inedible. In minute quantities it is not deadly, for Tom and I have at times included small greenish areas in the salvaged slices.

But one of my most lyrical science popularizers speaks of the "unwholesome byaline threads of the black bread mould," and I cannot be sure that the byalinishness, whatever that is, does not extend to green. Our science-martyr complex is so weak that we have never eaten it in quantity. As for me, although I have no longer that sublimely heartening sense of indispensability I used to have, still, having survived my very brief heroic age with little damage except the minor matter of atrophied ideals, I cling most illogically to existence. In other words, I do not risk my precious hide if I can help it.

There was little time to mourn over mouldy bread. Enchanting as the point was—and is—we must be getting along, especially since our experience with trolling had been so disappointing. There undoubtedly was good fishing, if one knew where to fish, and I had no doubt that, given time, we could find the fishing. But time was not given; it was very sparingly lent. We had already spent our ninth night in the bush, counting in the half-night at Radiant. We had only five, or at most six, left. We must be on to Hardy Bay and the Glory Hole. Moreover, I wanted to be over the open stretch before any high wind should happen along.

We were at the extreme north-east corner of the lake, and Hardy Bay is at the extreme south-east. Part of the route lies directly along the eastern shore of the lake, but the distance is greatly shortened by cutting across an extensive bay. Beyond this, a long, rather narrow channel, with several islands, leads to Hardy Bay, into which Dickson Lake empties through a tiny connecting channel three or four hundred yards in length.

It may have been ten o'clock when we set out for Hardy Bay. We trolled, of course, but without hope, since we were paddling at fair speed. Even so, we caught one and lost two before we left the lee of the two heavily-wooded islands which lie near the shore and extend to the beginning of the big bay. We caught also the branches of a recently submerged tree, and after half an hour counted ourselves lucky to rescue both troll and lure. We should have kept the troll in then, but the insane fear of leaving a fish behind drove us to let it out again. Just at the moment when we lost the shelter of the last island, and began to realize that the breeze was increasing in strength, there was a fierce tug on the line. It was no tree this time, no rock; it was undoubtedly a fish.

For one moment I thought of turning back into the protection of the island to land our catch in quiet. Then back over my right shoulder I looked up the expanse of Lake Lavieille, stretching far north-west to a dim and dour horizon. The sky was dull, and here and there traces of white were showing on the water surface. A bit of foam floated by the canoe. I shivered, and began to paddle harder. Tom responded, and the canoe shot ahead.

I supposed that the fish would in some way get off, and as the wind continued to rise, I hoped fervently that it would. I had no desire to be engaged with a fish and a storm at the same time. But that fish did not get off. It jerked at the line with disconcerting frequency, and since I had no idea of its size, except that it must be a huge brute, to keep up such a struggle, I was afraid that one herculean heave on its part might coincide with a toppling billow and send us over.

After what seemed an eon of time, but was actually twenty minutes, we crept within the shelter, not very impressive, but adequate, of the first low islands, little more than reefs, that form the entrance to the long channel leading to

Hardy Bay. The water was very shallow along here. We were contentedly slowing down, when the fish gave a jerk on the line. I had almost forgotten it. That fish was still out beyond the lee, and we might well become snagged on a submerged rock out there. The thought of being forced to go back into that sea was too terrifying. I began to reel in frantically and shouted to Tom to paddle hard. He did so, and of course we soon found ourselves circling back to the open. Poor Tom had to paddle furiously on the other side, and with this unlovely zigzag movement we worked our way along the island. Past it, the channel deepened again, and in this now peaceful water we began to enjoy the situation.

Our fish was no giant, after all, though of good size. It was a speckled, not a lake trout, and the largest speckled trout we had taken. We let the troll out, and almost immediately had another strike. With six, four of them lake trout, we desisted, though the temptation to continue was almost too strong to overcome. This was our first successful trolling, and we began to feel that trolling might be admitted as a form of genuine fishing.

Buffeted, tired, hungry—but not for fish—we came to a moss-covered, sloping point with a pine stump ready waiting on a tiny semi-peninsula, and decided to lunch. I scarcely know why the memory of that spot is so fragrant to me, but I can understand why Tom regards it with affection. He caught, less than two hundred yards away, the biggest trout of the whole expedition. Like the bracken-covered point on Lake Mallic, just past the roughest part of the Creek travel, this Arcadia derived much of its charm from the contrast with the heaving waters we had left not half an hour before.

Most of my friends despise cosiness. They regard it as

unheroic, sentimental, non-virile. They consider cosiness as synonymous with stagnation and bovine placidity; they see a green slime on the surface of cosiness. They find it non-significant, reactionary, bourgeois, academic, Victorian. They define cosiness, or would define it, as spatial escapism, as claustrophily. In point of fact, not one of them has the word in his working vocabulary.

Hence, I shall not call this a cosy spot. It is merely a small open area, strangely free of undergrowth, though the shrubbery around it is dense. It has two old pine stumps, a small one in the open space itself, a larger on the edge. Blueberry bushes there are, and a dozen pine seedlings. It might be a hundred feet square, if it were anywhere near square.

Here was one noon fire that did not call for haste. An hour's paddling in sheltered waters, an insignificant carry at the end of Hardy Bay—this was all that lay between us and our next camp at the lower end of Dickson Lake; not two hours' work in all. We could indulge ourselves, like Parkman's Ojibwa fisherman, in a lazy luxury of idleness. There was only one obstacle to complete contentment. The fish! We had to eat them all. At the end of Hardy Bay is a trout hole so teeming that it has for many a long year been known as the Glory Hole, and we must not spoil the perfection of our fishing enjoyment there by any left-over catches. Even Tom appreciated this situation, and promised to do his duty, if he bust.

I cleaned the fish while Tom built the fire and put on the tea and dishwater billies. I filled the frying-pan with trout and cooked them. We ate them. I filled the frying-pan again with trout and cooked them. We ate them, Tom with groanings which he constantly uttered. I filled the frying-pan a third time with trout and cooked them. I called upon Tom to come and get his share, but in vain. I entreated; I admonished. I appealed to his better nature, to his sporting instincts, to his regard for his plain word. I drew his attention to the hideous fate to which he was consigning me. I ate all the fish in the third full frying-pan myself.

Since we had taken five large trout in the channel, and all within half a mile of this point, there was no doubt of our ability to catch more. Nevertheless, as we paddled away from that idyllic nook, there was no suggestion made of risking a troll. Even the thought of the Glory Hole made me shudder.

Down the channel, which widened in places between its high shores, and divided finally to pass to right and left of the last, lofty island, we paddled, and came out at last into the open of Hardy Bay, from the far side of which the giant pines towered so far above the general level of the forest trees as to dwarf them into the appearance of mere undergrowth.

I have no knowledge of the happy chance that spared those big pines when the great lumbering operations were being carried on, over half a century ago, but there they stand, or stood, nearly a hundred and fifty of them, on the narrow ridge separating Hardy Bay from Dickson Lake. Tom was duly impressed when he discovered that what he had taken for low undergrowth was really very decent average forest, and that the trees towering here and there far above were virgin pine. We interrupted our journey to land on the shore near one of them. We did homage to them, and measured their girth with pieces of string tied together—fifteen and a half feet for some of them—and marvelled at the tremendous thickness of the great ridged bark. We speculated with abandon about their height and their age.

They were too huge to be treated as friends. If we had lived when these were only average pines, it would have been possible, I suppose, to establish comradeship with them. They were not monstrous, as if their pituitary glands had misbehaved; they were god-like. Since I was born after the great ravaging, I need smaller trees, about two feet in diameter, for chums. For, with a diminishing faith in mankind as a species, with an impaired faith in animals for reasons which will appear later, I have been driven back upon trees. Unlike Whitman's animals, trees are respectable, but they are as far above human respectability as the animals are. They have infinite individuality, especially if isolated, when their individuality becomes at times eccentricity. Untroubled by introspection, taking no thought for their stature, they grow serenely, steadily, without envy or malignity or sense of inferiority. They are not effusive; they do not try to do you good, nor do they try to expand their ego at your expense.

In return for this inoffensiveness, this lack of the greedy aggression found in the diseased animal will, the trees have been permitted greater differentiation of healthy personality. A normal animal must be content with four limbs; no such restriction is placed upon the branches of a tree. Possibly, when man has attained the trustworthiness of the tree, he may be allowed its freedom. I have read and been told that the chief difference in constitution between hemoglobin, in the blood of animals, and chlorophyl, the blood of plants, is an atom of iron in hemoglobin over against an atom of magnesium in chlorophyl. This gives me hope. Man, a little lower than the tree, may some day deserve the atom of magnesium. In the meantime, I can approach a solitary tree with pleasure, a cluster of trees with joy, and a forest with rapture; I must approach a solitary man with caution, a group of men with trepidation, and a nation of men with terror.

The Glory Hole is at the upper end of Hardy Bay, near the little channel, at that time still obstructed, through which the waters of Dickson Lake find their next level in Lavieille. I pointed it out to Tom, just before we reached the portage. As we should be fishing there later, we left the canoe at the beginning of the trail. Since that time the channel has been cleared. We—Tom and I—no longer care, because, as I mentioned in another connection, there is now a ranger's cabin on the Dickson end of the trail, and for that reason we shun the place as if it were a garden party.

At this time, however, it was a deservedly popular camp-site. A pleasant path, redolent of pine, led to a spring of water achingly cold. The tent itself snuggled among fragrant cedars. Much usage had cleared the camp-site of undergrowth and weeds, and had provided a chip-pile of respectable dimensions. The cleared area was quite small, and the dense forest crowded closely in upon it. To the south lay Dickson Lake. The shore at this point is low, and the camp nearly as low as the lake level.

We reluctantly decided to postpone fishing until after we had eaten. The evening was to be given over to the ecstasies of the Glory Hole, and we wanted no impending meal or dishes to tarnish its splendour. While we were washing the dishes, by the way, we discovered that again the household soap had been left behind, at the idyllic lunch spot. We debated going back for it in the morning, but we had put Lake Lavieille behind us, and entrancing as it was, we could not go back. We cut Tom's half cake into two pieces, each taking one for his personal toilet. The other half of Tom's soap we now devoted to the household. We also passed a by-law that the man next responsible for losing the soap should forgo its use for duration.

Then we went to fish the Glory Hole. It is contained in a deep little pocket, the shore is darkly wooded, and its opening is toward the west. The sunset that night was full of solemn, gorgeous pageantry, fraught with weather prophecy, could we have interpreted it. But, as you may already have guessed, the sunset splendour was all the glory we were to have that evening.

We waver between two explanations of our failure to catch any trout in the Glory Hole. The first arises from our simplicity. Concerning the veracity of humanity in general we agree with the Psalmist in his haste, but we accept the most careless statement of a fisherman, not with polite assent, but with enthusiastic and unquestioning belief. Consequently, as I have already said, we are convinced that all our predecessors at any given fishing spot have been almost incredibly successful. Now a sufficiently long succession of almost incredibly successful fishermen would exhaust even the Glory Hole, and our first explanation is that we were the first to arrive after the final depletion. The second is more sinister. We may not have fished the Glory Hole at all. We may merely have fished a hole in the water, just a hole. The sinister aspect of this becomes clear when I inform you that my knowledge of the Glory Hole rests entirely on Jim's information. Jim showed me a place, and said,

"This is the famous Glory Hole you've heard so much about."

Now I had never heard of it in my life until he had mentioned it himself two or three days before, but I had immediately become excited about it. For whatever value it may have as evidence, I might add that Jim and I had caught nothing in the Hole. When Tom and I took our eleventh perch, I suspected Jim of having hidden the Glory Hole from me, probably in fulfilment of some solemn oath to earlier proprietors, and of having palmed off on me this perch resort.

The amazing feature of it was that Tom insisted on keeping a dozen or so of the perch, protesting that he was extravagantly fond of all fish but trout, which he now classed as coarse stuff. He also assured me that perch were never wormy in June, no never. These were. After the taking of the perch I admitted miserably to myself that the lazy creatures we had seen in the quiet part of the channel between Hardy Bay and Dickson Lake had really been suckers. Up to this time we had seen nothing but trout and minnows. Nothing but trout had molested our bait, so far as we knew. I think we had both developed a naive belief that trout were the only fish inhabiting these waters. Hence I had declined to accept the presence of suckers, even when visible to the indignant naked eye.

The sunset beauty ended somewhat abruptly, and we pulled in to shore. In accordance with our fixed procedure, we had made our beds before setting out to fish. Our night tasks were done. I was able to persuade Tom, after examining three or four of the perch, that he did not want any of them cooked. We smeared on a new layer of fly-dope and, sitting silent on a log at the edge of Dickson Lake, we gazed to the south up the dark loveliness of that lonely water. We had been sitting not more than ten minutes when Tom stood up abruptly.

"I'm going to start the fire up," he said.

I had begun to feel the same way. For the first few minutes, the intensely solitary mood of the lake, especially as seen from our log by the shore, had been full of healing and calm. It had induced a denuding of personality that was inexpressibly refreshing. That had been followed, for me at any rate, by a poignant impression of invitation, of calling, into that infinite remoteness. Suddenly, something in the quality of that calling had brought upon me a quite irrational condition approaching panic. It was very silly, of course. There stole into my mind a fragment from an old Uncle Remus tale.

"It bad w'en de ha'nt holler, w'en de ghos' call. You call, dey don' make no answer. W'en dey call, hol' yo' mouf shet. It bad to make answer w'en de ha'nt holler. Dey call-a you 'way fum dis lan'."

Then I came to, and was able to laugh at myself. Nevertheless, I had an intolerable craving for something close and friendly and companionable. Tom's fire had surely been his response to a similar need. I followed him up from the shore and watched him coax a flame. In another five minutes I should not have required it, for the loons began, though, as if subdued by the insistent solitude, they soon became quiet again. At intervals, however, irregular enough to be thrilling, the far-off, lone cry floated through the dusk.

Our fire was not a big one. Wood was too far to carry to waste riotously. Moreover, a huge fire is not companionable; it is very literally repelling. It separates its devotees from itself and from each other. It conveys a sense of excitement, of dramatic activity, which may meet the demands of a crowd, but is alien to the spirits of a small group in the bush. At any rate, it is alien to the spirit of us two.

To the man who has preserved the boy's imagination, or who can recover a portion of it at such times, the contracting universe of a nightfall fire offers a rich experience.

I suppose that adult reflection can find philosophical values in the symbolism of that same experience, but there can be little of the child's joy in such reflection.

When we sat down by Tom's fire, the shadows had lost their sharp outlines, but all objects were still individual. In a few minutes the outer boundaries of things began to fade, and the horizon shrank to within half a hundred yards. As the night deepened, and the horizon contracted, and the surrounding trees were lost in blackness, we became aware of little cracklings that were not connected with the fire. All the old stories I had heard of wild animals around a trapper's camp-fire came crowding back to me. It was easy to imagine a circle of watchful forms just beyond the reach of our firelight, and all the creatures which by day we wished to see found themselves quite credibly among them. As for deer, we took a dozen for granted. Wolves, bears, lynxes—why might they all not be peering in at us? Tom saw at times the hopeful beginnings of eyes. Neglecting the obvious loophole afforded by the possibility of one-eyed unfortunates, he was unable to accept single gleams, and spent his time vainly in looking ceaselessly and keenly about for pairs of reflections. We sat very still, listening and watching, moving only to put a stick on the fire, to relight a pipe, to listen more intently toward a sound.

Thus we crouched, a teeming world about us, long after the night had closed completely upon us. At last we allowed the fire to die down. The great wall of almost palpable blackness crumbled away as the fire subsided, and the circle vanished. Objects dimly reappeared. We could have built up the fire and restored the wall of blackness, but not the boy's mood. As a matter of fact, I suspect that Tom wanted to try it again, for he put on two sticks before we retired into the tent.

It was too late for cribbage, and in any case we had no desire to play, because we were still inwardly attentive to the world we had conjured up outside the black circle. This phantom world was dissipated by the expulsive power of a new magic, the primeval magic of Tom's two sticks, for when I blew the candle out, a dancing medley of forms played on the tent, set in motion by the renewed vigour of the fire outside. In a short time this silent dance was done.

There was still one little act on our programme for the night. We were not sleepy, and when Tom announced that he wanted to bring his diary up to date, I remembered a bit of essential mending to be done to my breeks. We lighted the candle once more and set to work on our respective jobs. A scratching close to the tent startled us to alertness. There was the soft crack of light feet on still lighter twigs, followed by silence for two or three minutes. I was about to speak when we heard it again. After a time we localized it in front of the tent. Tom began very carefully to undo the tent-fly. Judging that he intended to open it suddenly, I trained the flashlight on the opening-to-be. When he threw back the fly, we saw our visitor sitting upright on a small log not a foot from the tent, and facing us. It scurried off with a sharp squeak into the protecting darkness. It was only a young groundhog—a paltry representative for the bears and wolves and lynxes—but we were satisfied. We laughed, flytoxed the tent anew, and went happily to sleep.

We wakened to a leaden morning, sticky with humidity and animated only by myriads of excessively active mosquitoes. The fire sulked. Even the small pieces of dry branches that I broke across my knee cracked apart dully. There was no life in anything. The lake was grey, and the sky. Dispirited by all this and by the deep disappointment of the Glory Hole, we tacitly assumed, in the undiscussing manner in which so many of our decisions were made, that we were moving on. While we had been paddling over from Arcadia, I had thought of remaining in this pleasant camp for two days, but all that seemed folly now. I wondered what I had ever seen in the place.

Listlessly, after breakfast, we took down the tent and did up our bundles. With growing lassitude we brought the canoe up from the Hardy Bay end of the trail. Languorously, and in a primitive fashion, we put out our fire, looked about to see if we were forgetting anything, and pushed off.

In about ten minutes it began to rain, not in any tempestuous manner, but in that quiet, methodical way which suggests that there is no hurry, since all the day is to be devoted to this one job of raining. We should, of course, have recognized the symptoms, but had not done so. The very quality in the atmosphere which should have warned us of the imminence of rain had deprived us of the mental vigour, not very great, needed to recognize the signs.

I do not like to get wet in a canoe. On land, on any trip in the bush, I do not care very much, but in a canoe my whole being revolts against it. I desire greatly to be quite dry. Even the occasional splash from the other man's inexperienced paddle is unwelcome. Now on this occasion the one craving of my being conflicted with a still more imperative necessity. The stuff must be kept dry.

In these days we carry slickers, but at that time we had nothing which would shed rain except the groundsheets. We had left them out of the bundles, and since they were more than enough to protect the dunnage, we made what use we could of this surplus. Tom, in the bow, tied an end of his sheet around his neck, and trailed the rest of it behind him over the bread. Thus his back was protected. He insisted that he thought it prime fun to be rained upon, and found high entertainment in his sodden knees. I had my knees well covered by my sheet, which then extended over the blanket bundle, but the rain coursed down my back and shoulders.

The laying out of such shelter requires engineering skill of no mean order. Your ground-sheet must not be tucked in cosily around your dunnage. If it is, all the rainfall caught in that area drains into the canoe, with unhappy consequences. If, on the other hand, it is left to hang over the gunwale, it will soon be dragging in the water. It must be so disposed as to provide a good drainage basin, together with reasonable stability of position. This stability is difficult to maintain when one end of the ground-sheet is tied about the neck of a man paddling.

Tom was, of course, quite right. We did enjoy it. The adjustment resembled that of stream-fishing without waders. We did not wish to become wet, but once wet, we could laugh at fortune in that one particular. It was not so cold, and it was quiet. I think that I appreciated this last condition more than Tom did. The rain splattered down, making miniature craters and tiny explosions as it struck the surface; it traced out bizarre, streaked patterns running crazily hither and thither over the lake; it pattered on the ground-sheets in an entrancing rhythm based on a scale of beat-strengths, a rhythm in perfect harmony with the long, coarse measures of the paddle strokes.

Two fragments of popular songs of forty years ago, one of them obscure, but both insistently associated for me with rain, came singing to me across the years, and I hummed them, low, to myself.

> *I remember you! Yes, you bet I do!*
> *Wasn't you the feller with the open umbereller,*
> *That I met one rainy day upon the Avenoo-oo?*
> *I remember you!   Bet your life I do.*
> *Gee! I'm awful glad I met you;*
> *Bet your life I won't forget you!*
> *I remember you.*

Some connection with rain is observable in this. The obscurity lies in the second, a reminiscence, equally aesthetic, of the cake-walk era.

> *Then when we goes a-walkin'*
> *Why, we sets the people talkin',*
> *We's the winnahs every time.*
> *An' she says she is my honey,*
> *An' she uses all my money:*
> *An' I love her, yes, I do.*
> *I calls her Sadie,*
> *An' she's a lady!*
> *And I love her so, so, so!*
> *And I love her; yes, I do!*
> *I calls her Sadie,*
> *An' she's a lady.*

Over and over I sang them, to the gentle little tom-toms of the rain. It did not disturb my companion, because he was engaged on his own repertoire, not quite so ancient as mine, but equally bad. He was singing something that thought itself funny, and that introduced the refrain with a line running thus:

> *And this is how he whistled this tune.*

His alternative song was a thoroughly sentimental ditty

which seemed to employ the phrase "Down in the valley" every second line.

Thus, very happy, very wet, we paddled up Dickson Lake. Past the nearest island, by the two little islets on the left, up the channel between the mainland and the lake's one big island, then round the sharp elbow in the lake, where we must swing to the left, and the water grows shallow.

At last I abandoned my two old songs for one much more recently learned, from *The American Song Bag.*

> *I sail over the ocean blue,*
> *I catcha da plenty of feesh;*
> *The rain come down like hell, like hell,*
> *And the win' blow thro' my wheesk.*
> *O Marian, my good compan. . . . .*

Memory flowed sadly back to the donor of the book, and the boisterous occasions when we had shouted that song out together. When I think of him, I feel ashamed of having given the primacy even to trees. When I think of him, I repent my distortion of the text a few pages back, and I restore it.

> *For thou hast made him a little lower than the angels.*

The man who has been honoured to know four or five, or one or two, such as he was, cannot despair of humanity.

The immediate application of this last song was not apparent. We were trolling, of course, but in a perfunctory sort of way. There is a spot somewhere along here which gave Jim and me some good fishing, but I have not been able to find it again. We had one strike as we crossed the mouth of a bay at the bend of the lake, but failed to hook the fish. It was a big one, naturally, and I made a mental note of the place. I think we did go back there, but without any luck.

It must have been well on in the day when we reached our island. I was hungry. I had eaten half a chocolate bar, somewhat soft and oozy, because it had been in a pocket of my shirt and I had become warm. Having forgotten to keep both tin cups out of the dishes bag, we had passed the one cup back and forth on the blade of a paddle.

A golden, ridged sand beach falls away almost imperceptibly along the north-east side of the island on which we were now to camp. Only by worming our way around were we able to paddle close to shore, and to nose in behind the exposed roots of a cedar that curved out over the water. I was stiff and aching from keeping the same cramped position in the canoe, and nearly upset it in my disembarking clumsiness. All the exaltation of joy and sadness was gone. It is fun to paddle in the warm rain, if one's packs can be kept dry, but it is no fun to make camp in the rain.

Not until we were carrying the tent up the bank, over the huge, rotting, fallen trunk, down the path and past the two sentinel pines did it occur to me that we had been carefully protecting it from the rain, while we were being rained on ourselves. On that wind-swept island, camp must not be made where it would be too much exposed to tempest. For that reason we pitched the tent well back from the point, between two trees, and pegged it down with second-hand pegs, left perhaps by the Detroit doctor whose name is carved on the split-log table top. Our camp was uncomfortable in prospect. If there is anything I dislike more than any other non-catastrophic circumstance on a camping trip, it is a wet tent-bottom. We pulled up the drippiest of the little trees inside the tent, and the biggest of the growth in general. But at best it was wet. Not that we feared any of the legitimate fears of dampness and chills and what not. It was merely that we abhorred the idea of wet within the tent. We regarded the tent as our refuge from the fury of the elements and the insects. Wetness was one of the elements. Accordingly, we viewed our floor with extreme distaste.

Using one ground-sheet to cover what we were carrying, and the other to shelter what was still to be carried, we transported our goods from canoe to tent, and once more established domicile, in our first wet camp. We hauled the canoe part way up the bank and turned it over, with the worms and the tackle placed carefully underneath. For some reason or other, it now seemed necessary to defend our lines and rods and landing-nets from the cruel downpour. Once on land, we regarded the pleasant, placid and musical rain of the paddling hours as an alien monster.

We decided not to build a fire. Inside the tent, with the ground-sheets spread out, and our blankets—dry as toast—partially unfolded, we ate our meal. Bread and butter, a quarter of an onion each, some chipped beef, a spoonful of strawberry jam.

The steady pounding of the rain upon the canvas continued until six o'clock. Then we began to be conscious of individual beats. Soon these ceased, and we heard only the intermittent, heavy drops of water falling from the branches of the trees. The rain was over. We peered out, to see a dripping world, and the leaden sky breaking up in the west into shades of grey, through the lightest of which a small ragged patch of blue began to show.

"How about getting a fire going out on the point?" I asked.

"Okay," said Tom. Then, "Fine!" said Tom.

THE ISLAND OF THE PINES

CHAPTER X

THERE WERE really four significant experiences about that camp—the minnows, the leeches, the red squirrels, and the sunset. To be sure, there were the trees from which we have named the island—two columnar red pines which stand at the beginning of the point proper and serve as entrance pillars to the dark, chambered depths of other pines behind. But they take on the eternal aspect of substantial verities, and are not to be confused with these accidentals.

The minnows come into the story in the manner following. On the first morning after our arrival at Lavieille Dam, Tom had gone down after breakfast to the water's edge to clean out the porridge billy. When he came up, he asked me if I would care to vary my bait with minnows. At the moment I felt no need for them, but was interested in his story that they were flocking to eat the porridge as it lay on the bottom, and that, indeed, they were attacking it valiantly as it settled.

Later, we had decided to try minnows for bait. Tom had gone to work systematically to catch them. With mosquito netting and string he had rigged up a primitive sort of dip-net, about five feet by three in size, with each side fastened along a six-foot pole, and one end weighted down with heavy sinkers. The two extra feet on each pole served as handles. Armed with this, we went down to the water. A rock and a tree-trunk fenced off a little pool, and into it we dropped some rolled oats. Within a minute or two a few scouts had ventured into the pool, and almost immediately afterwards the main body swept in and assaulted the still descending flakes of oats. We lunged with our net behind and under them, and brought it up, quite empty. Not a minnow was in sight. We waited three or four minutes, until we thought they might have recovered from the terror; then we dropped another small handful of oats. Again the scouts, again the magnificent sweeping movement of the main body. Again the lunge, again the empty net. Not until we had tried half a dozen times did we admit that our method was much too slow and clumsy for such nimble creatures. By this time, too, they had become wary. They would return, but they fled at the slightest movement.

We tried a new scheme. We allowed the net to sink to the bottom and rest there, in the quite reasonable hope that they might eventually grow careless, lulled into a false sense of security by the harmless thing lying motionless below them. They did not grow sufficiently careless to let us catch them in that way.

By this time, we were more concerned with catching minnows than we were with catching trout. It was no trick to catch a trout, but it was apparently a feat to catch a minnow. We matched our wits against their wits, and I must confess that on the whole the minnows were the wittier. We did catch half a dozen. That is to say, Tom caught them, with a smaller one-man net of the same material. They were not particularly effective as bait.

Still, we could not help believing that they would be excellent bait anywhere else. Before we left the big Dam, Tom had by dint of tremendous stalking captured nine of the minnows, to be taken with us as bait for the lake monsters. Realizing that the water in which they were to be transported must be changed often, we had put them in a billy, from which, at intervals of about five minutes, we poured them into a second billy, filled with fresh water. By this means we carried them safely, all but one, to Hayes Point. There, in the interval between two showers, we prepared a splendid aquarium for them. Securing the two poles of the large and unsuccessful minnow-seine to the bank, we suspended the net between them in such a way as partially to submerge it in the lake. Into this self-changing water we dumped our minnows. When, however, the storm over, we went down to select some for trolling bait, we found that the net had been disarranged, one end of a pole had sagged below the surface, and the minnows had escaped. Two only remained. They had been caught in the meshes of the net and had been drowned. They were quite dead. In fact, as far as minnows are concerned, my experience has been that if they are dead at all they are quite dead. Oblivious of the fate we had intended for them, I felt sad that the two had not escaped with their fellows. These latter had travelled perhaps fifteen or twenty yards, before falling a prey to the voracious monsters of the deep in these parts. The waters around Hayes Point provide no proper nursery for young minnows.

Thus our initial attempt at domesticating minnows

for bait had failed. But the first morning after our arrival at the island, Tom came back from emptying the porridge billy with the announcement that the schools of minnows here were bigger, better, and hungrier than any at Lavieille Dam, and that, moreover, the terrain was admirably adapted to operations against them, on account of its shallowness and lack of refuges. He was eager to begin a campaign at once. The net was brought out once more, and once more fitted with poles. Clad only in running shoes, we waded out to the end of the island and moved down the north side, until we came upon our first school. Then the race began. The minnows tried to swim to sea; we tried to trap them before they could get out of reach. When we lifted the net the first time, we had twenty or thirty, all too small for our purpose, but within half an hour we had netted a supply of large ones sufficient for our needs for at least two days. Our minnow problem had been solved.

Then there were the leeches. I approach this subject with reluctance, and with a definite sense of shame. I understand that the fiercest joy of the camping trip is the cold morning dip. I know that it is an essential part of the ritual in the most indolent of summer camps. I am quite aware of all the lyric and elemental quality of that experience. But, alas, Tom and I know it not. If we go into the water willingly, it is only to wash ourselves, and only occasionally. The Creek is not inviting; it is cold, much too cold. As for the lakes, we can't swim. At this point we part company with almost all others who have ever gone into the woods for pleasure. I am conscious of the defect when I am in the bush. I envy my friends who splash in with brave ado, and splash out again, embodiments of health and cleanliness. I, too, want to splash in and come out of the foam like Aphrodite. I don't know about Tom.

Now, while the deepest satisfaction to be found in the bush arises from the sense of escape from the human and to the non-human, I cannot free myself entirely from the mesh of gregariousness. At most unexpected times, into the most isolated situations, there intrudes the influence of the social group, the restraint of the Social Contract. In the joy of playing a good trout at a picturesque spot, I will be deeply humiliated to catch myself wishing for a gallery. Consequently, when I noted, on the day of our arrival, the beautiful sandy beach north of the island, with the water deepening so gradually and so visibly that there seemed no danger whatever, I was seized with a desire to go bathing, not from any sudden urge toward cleanliness, but solely because I remembered joyous, mischievous groups of bathers on sunlit and moonlit beaches, banded in a glorious fellowship into which I could not enter. It was very silly, and I should have indignantly denied any such motive, had it been imputed to me by anyone else.

I do not suppose at all that Tom thought these thoughts, but he was willing to go in. We had an exhilarating, refreshing twenty minutes, and promised ourselves another swim in the evening, to be followed thereafter by three or four daily. Hence, I was surprised to hear Tom declare, when he came up from the point that evening with the teawater, that he was through with bathing at this place. It was alive with blood-suckers. In vain I insisted that there was no danger from them. Probably they would leave us alone, and even if one did attach itself to one of us for rations, a little salt would quickly enough detach it. I tried to shame him with allusions to intrepid swimmers in tropic waters who nonchalantly pushed man-eating sharks or avid crocodiles aside. For answer he invited me to come down and see for myself. He had scarcely exaggerated. The little sandy, pebbly point from which we took our cooking-water was teeming with the small brown-black creatures, ranging in size from tiny half-inch specks up to three-inch vampires. They were timid enough, in all conscience, but all the glory of that summer-resort beach faded away. We did bathe, but briefly, and in a business-like manner, with our loins, so to speak, girded for flight.

As for the red squirrels, I find it difficult to forgive them. They shattered one of my illusions about animals in the wild state, and left me only the trees. And I'll tell you why.

The sky cleared somewhat in the afternoon of our arrival on the island. The ground was, however, quite wet. Accordingly, when Tom, half-way to the camp-fire on the point with a loaf of bread, remembered something else to bring, he did not lay his loaf on the ground, but set it on the bottom of the overturned canoe, conveniently near at hand. On his return, a minute later, he discovered a red squirrel endeavouring to make away with the loaf. There was nothing disillusioning about this. Still, Tom was surprised at the boldness of the creature and as a precautionary measure went back and closed the tent. He thought it advisable, also, to put back into the tent our sadly depleted, still more sadly deteriorated, bag of bread, which we had hung outside on the tent-rope.

During our preparations for that meal and the eating thereof, we were captivated with the interest shown in us by the same red squirrel, which raced past our table, ran under it to cross from the pine on one side to the pine on the other, sat on a limb over the table and chattered, and once even ventured to run across one corner of the table itself, when we were both busied at the fire. At Tom's suggestion, we buttered a piece of bread—mouldy, I may say—and, placing it on the corner over which the squirrel had run, we retired from the table. The creature was nowhere within sight or sound, but in less than a minute it was on the table, had eaten the piece of bread, and had carried off a small chunk of cheese, not intended for it.

Before the meal was done, any traces of shyness had vanished. It would take bits of food from our fingers. Obviously, someone else had made a pet of it. The next day it would sit on our wrists and eat the smaller pieces offered to it. Larger ones it carried off and cached on branches of nearby trees. That first evening we used up precious camera film taking hasty and distant pictures of our visitor, fearing that at any moment it might revert to its natural wildness. Not it. By noon of the following day we could have easily enticed it to pose on the end of one of our noses, if we had wished to do so. On Tom's, that is; mine is too flat. We ignorantly named it Bill. We should have called it Beverley, or some other name common to both sexes.

This first evening was one of pure delight and wonder. When the squirrel first sat on Tom's knee and ate a fragment of chocolate without a trace of embarrassment, I was fairly mad with jealousy, quite uncalled-for, since immediately afterwards it came to me with equal freedom, not to say indifference. When we poured Klim into a tin cover, and Bill lapped it up with a miniature red tongue, we were in ecstasy. When Tom tied a small piece of buttered crust to the table, and the squirrel, after one tug, promptly bit the string in two, we stared at each other in incredulous amazement.

There was one slight annoyance. On returning to the tent with the food, we discovered, in the tent wall directly opposite the bread bag inside, a neatly cut round hole just large enough to admit a full-grown red squirrel without any discomfort. I felt that this was a poor return for our kindness, especially when no squirrel would have found the slightest difficulty in creeping under the bottom of the tent, ten inches lower down. We had to remember to stuff mosquito netting into the hole.

We still must stuff mosquito netting into the hole that squirrel made. Up in the bush it is inconvenient to mend the hole, since the tent is always either set up or rolled up. The setting up of the tent is the first job, before anything else is unpacked; the taking down of the tent is the last job, done after everything else is packed. As you can see, there is no opportunity in the bush to mend the hole. It might be possible to do the mending with the tent set up, but that is too much like sewing up the rip in your shirt with you inside the shirt. When we come out of the bush, the tent is opened up and thoroughly dried before being put away for the season, but by that time we are back into our town clothes, and the tent seems a big, clumsy thing. Now a man cannot spread it out on his lawn, and in the sight of all Israel squat down and put on a patch. Down in the cellar there is no room to spread it out. Tom doubts if the tent will ever be mended.

Still, this unnecessary vandalism on the part of the squirrel was not the cause of my disillusionment. After all, the smell of that bread was provocative, and the squirrel simply took the most direct route to the booty. The explanation of the disillusionment is found, as so often, in connection with property, and will involve some description of a parcel of land.

The point itself is very narrow, and quite high. For the last twenty-five or thirty yards it is not more than fifteen feet wide at the top. The table and fireplace are near the beginning of this final narrow ridge. I believe that it has been accurately surveyed. The reasons for this belief will appear presently.

On the morning after our arrival, Bill was on Tom's knee, busily but peacefully eating. Suddenly it bristled, sat up, and seemed to be listening. Then, springing to the table, it began to scold, and almost at once there was an answering chatter down the bank directly below us. Bill darted down the bank, and we could hear a brisk interchange, receding in the direction of the tent. In a few moments our squirrel returned to the interrupted meal, while from a young tree fifty feet away the baffled intruder raged vociferously against a quite indifferent foe.

Within the next two hours the incident was repeated, and again. The situation was by this time perfectly clear. By whatever means a squirrel acquires title, Bill had evidently taken possession of all the point, including the table and fireplace, and extending a certain distance beyond them. There could be no question of the value of this property. For instance, we were at this very moment enabling Bill to live a life of luxury, and indeed to put some by for a rainy day. Bill was, in fact, a bloated capitalist. The other squirrel was undoubtedly a Red.

The day was too windy for fishing, and we abandoned ourselves to watching the economic struggle, waged ostensibly for the protection of ancient property rights, but actually for the privilege of exploiting us and our foolish kind. It went on intermittently. We soon discovered that the area was occupied and disputed, not by two individuals, but by two families of squirrels. The one who owned us was at times compelled to relax her vigilance to attend to other responsibilities. The family tree, while close to the estate, was not actually upon it, and there were times when the property was left unguarded.

Tom had gone for wood, and I was sitting beside the table. There had been no sign of any animal for fully half an hour, and I had decided to go back to the tent. Turning slightly, I was startled to see a squirrel sitting not six inches from the elbow that was resting on the table. It was the trespasser. I knew that, partly from some slight difference in appearance, more from the difference in manner. With mixed feelings of sympathy for the under-squirrel and fear of being disloyal to the law, I slowly broke off a bit of chocolate, and laid it on the table. The squirrel paused irresolutely for a moment, then seized the chocolate, and retreating to the farthest corner of the table, proceeded to eat. There was a sudden stir, and blazing with fury, Bill seemed fairly to hurl herself upon the table. The two faced each other in silence for fully two seconds, and I thought that a fight was imminent. I had time to wonder what I ought to do in this delicate situation, whether or not I should offer to mediate. Then there was a sharp exchange of remarks, and with ludicrous precipitance the trespasser turned and fled. I think it was not cowardice, but the burden of guilt, that caused the flight.

Soon Bill returned from the pursuit. In order to clear myself from any suspicion of complicity with the enemy, I prepared some tasty offerings of food. She was not hungry, for she took them all and cached them on the little trees and shrubs near by. After that she disappeared, but I could hear her scolding down the bank and along the road to her home tree. Again all was quiet.

Tom came back. I told him about the encounter on the table, and we watched hopefully for developments. Twenty minutes passed without incident. Then the squirrel returned. Tom, of course, noticed it first. It was sitting on a branch, eating one of the bits so recently cached. As I discerned at once, it was not Bill, the original hoarder, but the trespasser, now an unabashed thief. Not satisfied with this single purloining, the rascal had searched for and found two more of the not very carefully hidden stores before the voice of outraged ownership came storming along the bank. The pilferer ran down the tree, scrambled across the ridge, and disappeared down the opposite side. Once again, and only once, did we see the intruder in the forbidden territory. Again it was eating in a tree in which we had seen the proprietor hide some of our supplies, but we could not be sure whether the loot had been stolen from the owner of the point or directly from us.

To confess the truth, we both hoped it had been stolen from Bill. From the time when I had seen that Bill was not in present need of food, and was not even burying it in approved fashion for winter consumption, our sympathies had gone over to the outlaw. Thus it was, too, that I was disillusioned with respect to animals. I had considered that only man, and domestic animals corrupted by evil human communication, would deny to others what they could not use themselves. When, on the day we left the island, we discarded enormous quantities of mouldy bread, we took pains to scatter it up and down the whole campsite in such a way that no one squirrel, no matter how energetic and acquisitive, could take it all into possession.

It was fortunate for us that the squirrels did provide a source of entertainment. As I said, the weather was bad for fishing. The wind had come up in the night, with sufficient vigour to arouse me. I lay awake and worried over the canoe, which was probably being tossed about by the gale sweeping across the point. After a while I got up and, flashlight in hand, crept out to rescue our craft. It was lying undisturbed exactly where we had put it, but I pulled it fifty feet farther up the bank and felt much better.

In the morning the storm was still blowing, and we had to build up a shield behind which to light our breakfast fire. When, about half-past ten, the squirrels seemed to have retired, we improvised various games, mostly of the duck-on-a-rock or quoits types, with essential local modifications. Soon after eleven there was a lull, and more from a strong sense of propriety than from any real enthusiasm, we decided to go trolling. The wind rose again before we were ready to troll, and delivered us from the necessity.

Late in the afternoon the wind dropped, and the early evening saw all the turmoil gone, with clouds enough left to ensure a sunset colourful but not too splendid for a quiet mood. Our dishes were washed, our beds made, our kindling and birch-bark ready for the morning fire, our prunes set to soak. The squirrels were silent and invisible. Not even a loon called.

We had been sitting on the ground, looking into the west, our backs propped against a big log not far from the fire. I turned away from the fading colour in the sunset to gaze into the sombre resignation of the forest behind our camp. In the full light of day, the massed foliage of the great pines and hemlocks, as seen from this log, kept the woods behind our two sentinels in mysterious and profound obscurity. Even the afternoon sun, which threw a sheet of sunlight against the wall of forest, only made the depths beyond more opaque.

But just before the sun settled below the toothed horizon beyond the lake, its slanting rays began to reach long fingers into the depths. Stately trunks far within the woods stood suddenly revealed, the strong, rugged patterns of their bark as legible as though a few feet away. A tiny pine, at the extreme tip of the longest finger, came startlingly into view. Even as we watched, however, the little pine drew back into the darkness, and the sunlight crept up the trees. In three or four minutes the light had moved up past the branchless lower trunks, and had disappeared in the massed resistance of the heavy foliage. Still two or three minutes, and only in the very tops of the two sentinels did the brightness linger. Then they too lost it.

Not until that moment did I recognize the source of poignancy in the beauty of that scene. As the light faded from the tops of the two pines, I realized that the trip was over. True, there were possibly three full days in the bush before we should load the canoe on the top of the car at Sproule Bay. But those would be only the days of getting out.

This moment comes always as a shock. We can never predict the time of its coming, because the instrument, not yet discovered in laboratories, wherewith the spirit detects and records it, is far too delicate for the clumsy consciousness, accustomed to the coarse, approximating measure of days and hours. Normally there is a definite time when we must be back on the treadmill, and our movements of the last three or four days are governed largely by that factor. Nevertheless, there is a clear divide. Up to that divide we have been forgetting, or trying to forget, that an end must come to freedom. We usually succeed in keeping the disagreeable thought of going out so far back in consciousness that it can emerge only momentarily as an unidentified discomfort. Then, at some incalculable point of time, our whole attitude changes. The trip is over. That accepted, we become eager to be out. The joy of loitering is gone. The delight of the eyes is past. Let's get home.

This is the last of our half-dozen moments. The first is the one that comes soon after New Year's, and drives a man down cellar to pore over his tackle. There may be a second when we are beginning our packing. A third, for the two of us at any rate, is on the morning of setting out. About twenty-five miles away from home the amazing truth breaks upon us that actually, after all these months of dreaming and planning and doubts of getting off this year, we are on the way to the bush and the trout. Another comes with the smell of the first camp-fire in the bush, still another when the first trout is taken. A solemn though artificial time arrives when we reach the more or less mathematical half-way hour, or when we round the geographical turn of the trip. Finally, the hidden moment that has just now come upon me, and upon Tom. Since I can never refrain from giving vent to my lamentation at this time, and hence communicate it to Tom, I cannot tell whether he experiences it independently or not. Probably he has his own moment, but—a much more taciturn person—he never tells his grief.

We discussed the times and the seasons. Not the route, for there was only one. A twenty-minute paddle across the lake into the little bay opposite the island. Then the Long Portage, not much over three miles, but generally referred to as the three-and-a-half-mile carry. Then tiny Bondfield Lake—a five-minute carry— Wright Lake, somewhat longer than Bondfield—a ten-minute portage—and the East Arm of Opeongo. After that, the fourteen-mile paddle down Opeongo to the car waiting for us at the foot of Sproule Bay. We hope it is waiting for us.

The Long Portage would be tough. We should take

over one load and make camp on Bondfield. Next day we should go back for the second load and move on to the East Arm. Then, stealing off in the early dawn, to be reasonably sure of a calm lake, we should do the last lap.

Sobered, we watched the night fall and the stars come out and the woods behind us grow black and the lake become indistinct. The fire went out. After a while we retired to the tent for our rubber of cribbage. It must have been late. Once there, the sense of a break faded to some extent, and the continuity was patched together again for an hour.

ALL OVER

CHAPTER XI

WE PACKED with particular care. There were two problems. In the first place, since we were facing the Long Portage, the loads must be made as easy to carry as possible. Hard little packages poking a man in the back could be tolerated on a half-mile carry, but not on three and a half miles. Fly-dope must be handy. The last chocolate rations must be divided. The stuff must be especially distributed for these two trips. The cooking gear and the table service generally go on the second, the canoe load, but this time they must be taken over first. The tent must not be packed until most of the dew had dried off. Water is heavy.

Approximately twenty minutes before we had finished packing, the wind rose. Dickson Lake, shallow in this part, was churned up into masses of white, across which it would have been folly for canoeists with our degree of proficiency to venture. A slightly earlier getting up, a bit less leisureliness in packing, the postponement of breakfast until we had crossed the lake—any of these would have set us on the long trail, where wind could mean only cooling breezes on grimy, sweaty faces. Now, we might be held up until night, or even until next morning.

Anxiously we watched for a sign of quieting. At half-past eleven, we had to unpack enough to cook a lunch. Then we waited some more. In mid-afternoon there was a slight lull. Grown desperate now, we loaded the canoe, and lying just inside the shelter of the island, we waited for a chance to make a dash across.

"What do you think, Tom? Can we make it now?" I asked, anxious that he should confirm my hope or at least share my responsibility.

"Just whatever you think. I'm willing," said Tom.

There was no use swearing at him. We waited a few minutes longer.

"Ready?"

"Okay."

We shot out from behind the end of the island. It was too rough for comfort, but not so bad as we had expected. One route gave us a good angle for paddling, but left us exposed practically the whole way. A second would carry us much more quickly into the lee, but gave us almost broadside wind while we were exposed. Nevertheless, uncertain of how soon the wind might be worse, we chose the second route and made for the nearest mainland point across the lake. It was only a short distance, and we had no real difficulty, but when we laboured into the shelter of the bay beyond the point, I was ready to take in my paddle and rest a minute. We looked back, hoping, of course, to see a wild sea tossing, but the wind had died away. By the time we landed, the lake was exasperatingly smooth. We had selected the last quarter-hour of the wind's activity for our dash.

The Long Portage now is a very different carry from the one we took that afternoon. A great lumber company, with a name famous for well over half a century in all the north country, has been exercising its timber rights. A sleigh-haul road runs from Dickson Lake to Bondfield, and the portage follows this road most of the way. At one place, twenty minutes from Dickson, the trail, turning in by the pig-pen, and swinging at a right angle over a bridge, just past the building used by the camp watchman in summer, becomes the main street of the lumber camp, with its neat row of log buildings. Aside from two or three detours, and the last ten or fifteen minutes of the Bondfield end, the trail, as I said, now follows the log road. These detours explain some of our lack of enthusiasm for the new route.

I have not the slightest doubt that the lumber company would expect gratitude from all campers who use their road, but even if the road were paved, and provided with escalators on the hills, there is only one feeling possible to campers who see the devastation wrought in their beloved forests by lumbering operations, and it is not gratitude. Lumbering of fifty years ago can be forgiven. Ruined camps, broken dams, rotting chutes, grass-grown tote-roads—these have a certain antiquarian interest of their own. There has been time, too, for the worst of the ravages to be repaired. It is astonishing how few years are required to bury a camp beneath a mass of green, partly grass, partly bramble, partly small trees. Even the second-growth trees are of respectable size, unless the slash has been burned over once or twice. But the raw desolation left by last winter's cut is a very different matter.

In any case, gratitude would be temperate, because these dual-purpose roads are seldom satisfactory to both parties. The lumber companies, in building the roads, seem to place their own selfish interest first. Now their purpose normally requires that a road be as nearly level as possible. There is nothing objectionable in this, except that the most level part of a given area in the bush is apt to be the lowest. This is all very well for the lumbermen, who do their hauling when everything is frozen solid, but it is bad for the poor camper, who comes along in sunny June and finds the road in many places a morass. Hence the two or three detours. (A detour is laid out when the leap from one hummock in the muskeg to another exceeds eight feet.) In another respect, also, the interests of the party of the second part are worse than disregarded. When the company builds its road through the swamp, it does not depend entirely on the frost, but proceeds to lay corduroy along the wettest places. Since there will be a layer of snow and ice between the corduroy and the sleighs, it is not laid with any too great regularity. Tom maintains that it is laid with extreme care: he swears that it is laid by a particularly malignant railroad-man, who has managed here to improve upon the hideous ingenuity displayed in spacing railroad ties so as most to impede the pedestrian. In places, too, the pieces are laid lengthwise, and in wet weather no intelligent insurance agent would issue an accident policy, at any premium, covering travel over this stuff. It must be admitted, in fairness to the lumber company, that the worst of this longitudinal corduroy is to be found near the Bondfield end of the old trail, and not on the log road.

But when we passed over this first year, there was no lumber camp, no log road, no devastation. There was only the long portage, beginning in one swamp and ending in another, over which we plodded, climbing up and down the maximum number of hills, clambering over rocks, sliding down wet clay into treacherous root tangles, rolling laboriously over huge logs, and crawling cautiously under trees breast-high across the trail, pulling boots off in clinging ooze, slipping with a thud and a grunt from small, wet, round, barkless logs. We paused at twenty-minute intervals, selecting high logs or rocks or banks against which we could rest our packs and ease ourselves of the burden without actually removing the loads from our shoulders.

We set out with unhappy anticipations, remembering the long trail up to the Forks, a trail a mile shorter than this one. In the meantime, however, the alchemy of the woods had been active. From the night of our arrival at Lavieille Dam, we had done no hard work until this day, but we were no longer the soft tenderfeet who had entered the bush at Radiant. When we reached the end of the trail, and saw tiny Bondfield, we were so little conscious of any fatigue that we regretted not having set out early enough in the day to give us time for the second load. Tom did this regretting aloud, and I agreed with him. Secretly, I was ready to make camp and call it a day, for I had some misgivings about an additional seven miles. In these later years, I may say, we regularly do both trips on the same day, without undue weariness.

We cleared a small area, just sufficient for the tent and an entrance to it. There was no camp-site here. By now we were so full of the idea of being homeward bound and in haste that we did not even play our bedtime rubber of cribbage. Breakfast, too, was business-like and matter-of-fact, and immediately after it we took the trail for the second load. It is an irrational experience, not shared, I suppose, by the sensible, that of finding the empty return trip of a double carry longer than the burdened carries themselves. A stroll along a trail on the way to a fishing spot is a delight, with the eye alert for all the teeming interest of the woods; the same trail, when one is returning for a load, is weary, flat, stale and unprofitable. We noted a few landmarks—a spring, a certain boulder, a particularly steep hill, a piece of leather strap that Tom declares is exactly eight minutes from Bondfield.

Before setting out for Bondfield with the second load, we marked a chip and tossed up to allot the first ten minutes on the canoe. Tom had volunteered, as he usually did, but it was better to leave it to chance. There was some slight advantage in being relieved of this first bit, but it was very slight, for while the swampy nature of the ground made the first spell awkward going, the balance was redressed by the succession of steep little hills on the second. Beyond that, I could not remember the trail well enough to anticipate the further effects of the initial toss. I won the toss and carried the canoe through the swamp at the beginning.

The mood of the second load is a cheery one, as compared with the mood of the first. During the carrying of the first load, a man realizes that he is not putting territory behind him. He must still come back and do the trail all over again. He must stub another toe, or the same one a second time, on that root near the spring. He must fill his shoes once more with mud when he slips off the wet longitudinal corduroy. He must put his other eye out when he stumbles against the broken branch on the big spruce just past the Killer hill. But after every difficult bit on the second carry, a man may look back in his mind, and comfort himself that that is that. When he has done half the distance, he is not oppressed with the thought that he has really covered only one-sixth. If he wishes, he may gloat over the fact that he has completed five-sixths. I can never snatch any joy from this five-sixths business, however, for while the one-sixth depresses, the five-sixths cannot elate me. I cannot think in sixths, anyway, without my tongue aching. This cheerier mood of the second load is restricted to the long carries, of course, for a portage of moderate length is all of it cheery, under good conditions.

I was trudging along on my third turn with the canoe, gleaning what satisfaction I could from the thought of this as the last load and indeed the last heavy carry of the trip. Tom was close behind me. Because, as I mentioned early in this narrative, I was behind the centre of balance when carrying the canoe, its front end was tilted somewhat downward. For this reason, I could see only a short distance ahead.

It is still a matter of inner controversy with me, whether I heard Tom first or not. I suppose it does not make any difference, but I wish I knew.

"Watch out!" he yelled.

"Woof!" something else grunted, emphatically.

I shot the front of the canoe up so quickly that the stern bumped on the ground behind and flew up nearly to horizontal on the rebound. Now I could see it, a large black animal thirty or thirty-five feet ahead, standing in the middle of the trail, and facing us. Here was Tom's bear at last.

A word about that "Woof!" The bear did not say "Woof!" Unfortunately, however, I have never succeeded even in an approximate reproduction of the sound a surprised bear utters. In the first place, I am a very inaccurate imitator of unfamiliar noises, anyway; in the second place, whenever I have heard that particular sound, I have always been as much surprised as the bear, and hence have lacked the calm, impersonal detachment necessary for good scientific observation. Some day I am going to cry "Boo!" to a well-chained bear cub, and then I shall dash at once to the piano and catch the notes.

In the meantime, all literary bears whom I have met, from Goldilock's three friends on, have apparently said "Woof!" and I merely follow the convention.

Although I had come across bears in the woods in earlier years, I had been wishing as ardently as Tom that we might see one on the trip. But I should not have selected the present circumstances, and I felt nervous, for the situation was not at all comfortable. Here I was, imprisoned under a canoe, and practically weaponless. True, I had my big knife, but I did not care for the close quarters involved in using it. The axe, in which I had far more confidence for this kind of work, was at the end of the portage.

The bear did not move when Tom came up beside me and whispered,

"Will I help you down with the canoe?"

"I wish you would," I answered, also whispering. "Let's ease it back to you. Watch him, and if he moves, stop still."

I knew nothing about the sex of the creature, but I wanted it to be a male. I had always understood that while a female with cubs was very formidable and irascible, the male black bear was ridiculously timid. She-bears in literature, whether oral or written, seemed never to travel without cubs. I knew that there must be times when even a she-bear would be free of maternal cares, but I was totally ignorant of ursine times and seasons. Accordingly, I willed that bear to be a male.

"Okay," said Tom.

Gently we eased the canoe back, until each of us was holding one of the two ends. Then we must turn it over, in order to let it down to the ground.

"Are you ready?" I asked, looking straight ahead of me.

"What did you say?" came in a stage whisper from behind.

"Are you ready?" I repeated, more loudly, but still without turning around.

"Sure," said Tom.

"Wait a minute," I said. I did not like to lose sight of the bear, just at the moment when our lowering of the canoe might be expected to precipitate any action he might think of taking. I suppose we stood thus for two or three minutes.

"Are you ready?" I asked again.

"Hell, yes," said Tom.

"Wait till I say 'Go,' and flop her over easy to the right."

"Okay," Tom replied.

"Let her down easy," I said. "Wait till I say 'Go.'—Go!"

Tom began to turn his end of the canoe as I had indicated, but in my excitement I forgot my own instructions and twisted to the left. As a result, the canoe remained above our heads, while two men racked it in an unpremeditated test of strength. Why the devil couldn't he follow plain directions? Then I remembered, and began to twist over to the right. Tom, of course, was now trying to turn his end to the left.

"Hey! What way do you want it?" he inquired, fiercely and not too softly.

"Left," I answered, but continued as I had been doing. "No, I mean right."

At this, Tom gave up the struggle and contented himself with steadying his end until finally my intentions became quite clear to both of us. The instant the canoe rested on the ground I looked up. The bear had not moved, but was watching us, apparently with some degree of curiosity. Tom came up beside me, and now for the first time I took a glance at him. He was radiant with excitement, pleasureable excitement.

"Say, I never thought we'd see a bear this far out," he said. "Damn, why haven't we got a camera here?"

Now that I was out from under that horrible canoe, I too began to enjoy the sight of the inoffensive creature. I had seen them before out in the wilds, but I had never met one on a trail until this day, and the experience was exhilarating. Nevertheless, I wanted to be on our way. I did not feel like urging the bear to get off the trail, however, nor did I see any way of making a detour, since the growth was too thick to allow us passage with the canoe.

Almost at the moment when I was about to ask Tom's

advice in the matter, the bear turned, and without undue haste left the trail and made its way into the bush. We stared after it, catching occasional glimpses of it through the undergrowth, until only the cracking of dry limbs betrayed its route.

Tom was so much uplifted and revived by this encounter, which he regarded as a delightful extra to the trip, that he rashly offered to carry the canoe the rest of the way himself, in order that I might have first sight of future bears on the trail. He evidently expected to meet them at frequent intervals on the way to Bondfield, and the prospect held nothing but charm for him. Tom had not been caught with a canoe on his head, as I had been. Not that I should have been disturbed at the appearance of another bear, for I took care I should not be surprised again. I had disconcerting reflections on what would have happened if I had unwittingly poked the end of that canoe into the bear's ribs; accordingly, during my turns I kept the front well up, and a clear view ahead. But nothing more startling than a family of partridges enlivened the rest of the carry.

By the time we reached Bondfield we were ravenously hungry, and full of eagerness. Tom talked incessantly about bears, and wolves. Three beautiful deer were feeding along the shore not far away; Tom paid no more attention to them than if they had been cows in a field. A moose might have interested him, but I doubt it. He had cast aside the lesser breeds, and demanded savage aristocrats. In fact, he wanted a pack of wolves, and I fancied I could detect a green wolfish flicker in his eye as he watched me eat my last pancake. But the flicker gradually died away.

We crossed Bondfield after lunch, and carried over into Wright. Stirred into momentary angling interest by a leaping fish in Wright Lake, we put out a line and made a good catch, accidentally legal because of a four-day advancement in the opening date of the bass season in that particular year. In the late afternoon we made camp under the pines on the East Arm of Opeongo.

Here was where our concern was greatest. We knew Opeongo only by repute, and that repute was formidable. Large areas of open water, big bays that must be crossed—these were indicated on the maps, and now lay visible before our eyes. Opeongo was a weather-breeder, a mother of storms, a place of sudden changes of air pressure. It was a malignant spirit, cunning, treacherous, the custodian of all the hatred against the encroachments of white men for three hundred years. For mediocre canoeists who were non-swimmers it was undoubtedly a big lake, especially big in such uncertain weather as we had been having. Quiet enough it lay now, in the evening glow.

It still lay quiet when, ten minutes after daylight next morning, we pushed off. Huge dark rolls of clouds were stretched across the sky. As the grey day opened up, we could see far down the lake the lighter break of an old meadow, probably a relic of the first lumbering days, the days of the old shantymen's song:

> *Come, cheer up, brave boys! We plough and we sow.*
> *And adieu evermore to the Opeongo.*

Somewhere, left of this meadow, was the channel into the South Arm. Half a dozen headlands we rounded, hopefully, and when we were sure that we had gone too far, the passage suddenly opened beyond an unpromising point, and we saw the South Arm spread out before us. Beyond its dark waters, the great hills stood half-revealed above mist-filled valleys. A white boathouse five miles away served now as a landmark, and we made our leisurely way toward it, past it, into Sproule Bay, past the ranger's cabin and the group of buildings near by, up the lazy creek, and to the wharf.

Two hundred yards up a sandy road the old car stood waiting for us.